T0247035

30-DAY
SHRED

a devotional
for reading the
ENTIRE BIBLE
in a month

NATHAN FINOCHIO

BroadStreet
P U B L I S H I N G

BroadStreet Publishing® Group, LLC
Savage, Minnesota, USA
BroadStreetPublishing.com

30-Day Shred
Copyright © 2024 Nathan Finochio.

9781424570225
9781424570232 eBook

Design and typesetting by Garborg Design Works | garborgdesign.com.
Editorial services by Michelle Winger | literallyprecise.com.

Printed in China.

24 25 26 27 28 29   7 6 5 4 3 2 1

ACKNOWLEDGMENTS

I want to thank Pastor Jude Fouquier for inspiring me to do this. Thirty-some years ago he was preaching at a youth conference in Utica, NY, and I had traveled down with my church from Ontario. He was seated for his session because he had dropped a weight on his toe in the gym. In his sermon he shared about how he had been reading the Bible—in its entirety—every month for three months. I distinctly remember thinking to myself, "I will do that one day."

I also want to thank the Alessi family for supporting the writing of this book.

THE SHRED

Why Shred?

My wife and I have a bunch of TV shows we watch together; in marriage you have to compromise on shows you both don't mind. I prefer watching straight-to-Netflix action thrillers with zero dialogue and stacks of bodies at the end. My wife is a cool kid with her European art house collection and Japanese anime arsenal. I'm not watching that noise—ever—and vice versa. So we settle for *Parks and Recreation*, *The Office*, and the occasional unsolved murder documentary.

Every now and then, she tries to introduce a show from her childhood into our canon—*Frasier*, *Friends*, and *Seinfeld*. The problem is, I didn't grow up watching TV; I was raised by two boomer pentecostal fundamentalists who not only didn't allow a TV in the house but were convinced sitcoms were written by Lucifer himself.

I've tried so many times to get into *Friends*; she's tried so many times to get me into *Friends*. But I'm not gonna start at the beginning because I'm not gonna watch 10 seasons of a half-funny sitcom (what a nightmare, sorry), and when she puts on an episode that is apparently hilarious, I don't get any of the jokes because everything is built on (you guessed it) prior seasons.

I don't have any context for the mild idiosyncrasies of the cast; I'm completely unaware of what could be a massive ongoing joke. Things that are being said and done go right over my head. So while the plot of the immediate episode might be understood, the weight of meaning understood by a hearer like my wife is unknown to me.

And this is how many of us read the Bible.

The first problem is that we haven't read the Bible from cover to cover, and we forget that it's actually a book—a record of salvation history—with narrative that brings context to the seemingly standalone episodes.

The next problem is that we have learned to read devotionally and almost exclusively this way:

consuming Scripture one verse at a time, in small bites, looking to meet our immediate spiritual or soul needs.

When you are constantly reading devotionally, it's a bit like the ice cream diet—you never end up getting steak because everything has to be quick and sweet to the taste. You become spiritually anemic. It's also like examining the leaves of a tree under a microscope. And there's nothing wrong with that, so long as you keep in mind the shape of the tree from where that leaf came. But that's just it: we miss the forest for the trees many times. We don't know the context of what's happening, the loaded terms the cast are employing, and much more.

The 30-Day Shred is a recovery of the memory of the major themes of Scripture; it's a re-acquainting with the lay of the land, so to speak. It's binge-watching a TV show so the journey of the show is fresh in your mind the entire time.

My wife and I have been watching a new Samurai show lately. But what made me furious was that the ten-episode season dropped a new episode every Monday. It took me over two months to finish the show. And the problem with that was simple: I was losing context. The writers of the show knew that, so they would do a recap at the beginning of every show. Have you ever seen that "previously on…" recap? It's annoying when you're binge watching the old season; it's helpful when you're stuck waiting a week between episodes.

The Bible doesn't have a "previously" recap every time you read, which means that you have to put in the work of remembering context. This is precisely why I read the entire Bible from cover to cover in 30 days every January. I found it incredibly difficult to maintain the context of Scripture in my head without first looking back at it frequently. The context of every verse isn't just the immediate context of the passage, it's actually the greater context of the Bible itself.

I also do this because I'm a binge-watcher and I love getting the whole story in one sitting. There's a new season of a show coming out this summer that we've been dying to see, but they are releasing one show every Monday. I refuse to play that game because I love context. So I'm waiting for the entire season to drop so I can savor the flavor to the max. This is what theologians call reading *canonically*.

When I read a verse in the New Testament, I am able to recall Old Testament passages that the New Testament author is referencing because I am all caught up on the context of the entire canon of Scripture. The New Testament is written in the context of the Old Testament. So the more I know the Old Testament, the more I can understand the New Testament!

Almost every time Jesus speaks, he recalls the Old Testament. In the book of Revelation there are 404 verses, but there are over 450 references to the Old Testament. You gotta know the whole Bible to know the whole Bible! The fancy term theologians call this cross-referencing in Scripture is *intertextuality*.

Think of a meme page. When you are browsing memes, you see so many cultural references, like Peter Parker pointing at Spider-Man, or David Beckham talking to Victoria Beckham. Knowing who Peter Parker and the Beckhams are informs the meme, even though they are repurposed comedically. If you don't know the meme template of Batman slapping Robin, then the irony of the meme may be lost on you.

Doing the 30-Day Shred is re-familiarizing yourself with the entire canon of Scripture quickly so you can understand the details of the entire canon of Scripture with the ease of perusing a meme page. You've put all that cultural work into watching every movie ever, and you are rewarded by understanding the memes.

But the Bible just sits there unread, and we scratch our heads on Sundays, or we jump to conclusions about the sermon because we only have a little piece of the puzzle. Interpreting Scripture is like doing a puzzle. A puzzle piece only has meaning in the context of the picture you are trying to construct. When I'm doing a puzzle, I'm constantly referring back to the image on the box. That helps me identify where the piece fits. Knowing that the piece means nothing without the picture, you've got a choice to make: shred, or be a lost little lamb on Sundays.

Since I've been shredding, all of a sudden, my ears perk up at repeated themes and emphasized words; I'm making the connections that the authors are trying to make. I'm laughing at their inside jokes. The idiosyncrasies of the cast aren't lost on me. I'm beginning to read with understanding.

The 30-Day Shred is a bit of a rebellious thing to do in the age of short-form media. It takes a couple hours a day. You're reading an ancient text. It becomes painfully clear that it's not all about you as your mind is pulled into the story of others.

How To Shred

There's a way to do this and a way not to do this.

First, you aren't going to read as slowly as you would other things. The major focal point of the Shred is the shape of the tree, not the details of the leaf. For some of you, this will be your greatest challenge. You'll feel like you're doing the Bible a disservice by reading this quickly. But you have to keep coming back to your intent: to take in all the *Seinfeld* seasons in a week so you get the major movements. Then as you watch standalone episodes at your leisure, you begin to notice things you've never noticed before.

You've got to read as fast as you can because it's a lot of reading, and you need to finish every day in order to keep pace. Reading quickly doesn't mean you're missing important things; it just means that you are paying attention to bigger things. G.K. Chesterton once quipped that big things have a way of hiding themselves better than small things, like how we thought the earth was flat for a long time.[1]

Your job is to find the big things that have been hiding from you in plain sight for years. Read fast so you can finish every day; if you finish your daily readings, you will finish the Shred. If you finish the Shred, you will have seen things on this quick bus tour of the Bible that you would have never seen otherwise.

If you get in a jam one day, and you don't have much time to read, it's better to skim and finish that day's reading than to start the next day with double the amount of reading, and then abandon the project because of how underwater you find yourself.

Second, if you see something, make a quick note and then move on. As I do the Shred, I see sermon ideas and connections to other passages I've never seen, or I get impressed by the Holy Spirit about something in my life. As this happens, I write it down and then keep going. By the end of the Shred, you should have some significant things to contemplate and study.

Third, don't read a paraphrase like *The Message* or *The Amplified Bible*—you don't have all the time in the world. Read something that gets to the point quick, like the NIV or the ESV.

Fourth, do this with friends. It's way more fun when the community is shredding together. There are tens of thousands of people who do this every January. It's wild. Another fun idea is to enlist your illiterate friends and make yourself feel superior to them when they drop out after day five. Or let them do the audio version and make fun of them for it.

Lastly, use this devotional to help prep you for the day's reading. I will give you some things to look out for every day. Because you have so much reading to do, I'm not gonna overwhelm you. But what I'd like to do is give you a brief overview that helps you make a bit of sense of what you're reading. It's like being on a cliff with binoculars and trying to spot whales, and I'm the old dude who comes over and says, "Look over here; this is the path they are generally taking."

If this is your first time shredding, let me tell you something: you can do this. It looks hard, but it ain't. You were designed for a sprint; you can do anything for thirty days!

Here's my last tip, and then it's off to the races for you: use all available time to shred. You take a train to work? Shred. Get as much done as you can. Break at work? Get off social media and shred. Watching Netflix tonight? Cool. Shred at the same time; you've seen *The Office* 35 times already. The more you do in the morning, the better chance you have of finishing every day. But take advantage. Shred on the treadmill. Shred while waiting at the doctor's office. Shredding is a lifestyle.

I use the Logos app on my phone to shred in ESV. I prefer ESV, but that's just me. I like using the Logos app because I can shred anywhere, and I do. I like highlighting things that I see and that's as easy as dragging your finger across the screen. I change the colors of my highlights every year to track what I'm seeing. My Bible looks like a unicorn exploded on it.

It is my conviction that God has designed the human soul for mountain climbing: we are made for challenges. So my prayer for you is that you meet this challenge of grazing upon the Scriptures with all your "heart, soul, mind, and strength."

GENESIS 1
⬇
GENESIS 42

The first of five books authored by Moses, Genesis forms the bedrock of the entire Bible. As you get deeper into your Shred, you'll see quotations and allusions to this book because of how formative the stories are. Almost all the New Testament writers make use of Genesis. Jesus pulls from it multiple times authoritatively as he deals with marriage, his return, and his identity as God.

So what major themes should you be on the lookout for?

Let's start out by telling you how not to read this book: don't read Genesis asking modern scientific questions about it. Instead, read this book thinking of Moses, sitting on a hill, trying to explain to millions of freshly freed slaves who the God is that set them free and why he did it.

Moses is also tasked with leading and forming a new nation—a nation unlike any that has ever existed in human history—one instructed by God himself.

These slaves came out of 400 years of Egyptian bondage and were tempted to worship the gods of Egypt. Yнwн must introduce himself as God over all the gods of Egypt—superior in every way.

So Genesis acts as an introduction to the God of the Bible as well as culturally formative narrative. Every nation has stories that shape the political posture and manners of life of its people.

Genesis is no different.

The stories of God's rejection of the nations at Babel and his choosing of Abraham sets the pace for Israel's identity in the earth.

Watch how kind and patient and generous God is to Abraham and his offspring. Notice the nature of the covenant God has with Abraham and his progeny: a deeply flawed and dysfunctional family.

Here are some massive themes in Genesis that you cannot miss!

1. It announces the coming of a Redeemer who will fix the fall of man (Genesis 3:15).

2. It shows us how the world begins to get worse, not better, after the Fall. Angels marry women? And create violent monster people? Yikes. God decides to actively restrain the human capability for sin in the flood narrative.

3. It shows us how humanity tried to work their way up to manipulate God (Genesis 11), but God comes down to one man who believed him to save the world (Genesis 12).

Finally, when it comes to the miracles in the book of Genesis—things that seem so impossible like a talking snake, a garden guarded by angels, a flood, the confusion of languages—you have a choice to make. Do you read these stories archetypically, meaning that they have certain universal truths to be gleaned from, but didn't really happen historically? Or do you read them with a demythologizing eye, suggesting that the supernatural elements may have appeared that way to the eye of the author or perhaps became tall stories: the result of telephone whispers? Or do you read it as the way the first audience all the way to Jesus and the apostles read it, in the spirit the human author seems to suggest: a recounting of stories that God himself told—and the craziest part is that all the supernatural parts are true?[2]

For me, personally, it's a lot more fun to read *The Odyssey* like it happened. But as an evangelical charismatic Christian who believes in a God who came back from the dead, I find it much more engaging to read like the stories are true. And I think reading this way makes me the intended audience for the ancient author—or even puts me in the mind of the author—who seems to really believe he is recording history.[3]

Ultimately, I'm reading this book to encounter the divine author—because as a Christian, I confess the dual authorship of Scripture: the human author and the Spirit. So as I read Genesis, I'm wanting to hear both. And hopefully I can do that by reading in such a way that honors both.

MAKE A NOTE

The second installment of Moses' five-part series, this is where the story starts to get personal for Moses, who is about to catch the reader up to his present.

What happens in Exodus becomes the primal piece of liturgy for all Jewish literature and life. Leading Israel out of Egyptian bondage is the core story. It carries as much weight and bandwidth for Israel as the death and resurrection of Jesus does for Christians.

Moses is a child of anxious times (how desperate would his parents have been to send a baby down the Nile River to protect him?), who providentially becomes an Egyptian prince; yet somehow, he's in a struggle to find his identity as a son of Abraham, a son of promise. The world is his oyster, but the call of God is like a storm on the inside of him, causing him to reject it all by faith (Hebrews 11:23-28). Imagine the paradox of God creating safety for a season and then demanding that very same provision be cast aside as if it's a great evil.

This is a major theme in the Bible. The Bible is full of paradox: two things that are seemingly opposed to each other yet when balanced, hold each other up. Write down where else you see the paradox of God's protection and provision as you read along.

Scripture is replete with "both and" narratives and teaching. As you read Exodus, you'll see a God who is full of mercy and yet eviscerates bad guys. Consider the paradox of Pharaoh hardening his heart and yet God is hardening Pharaoh's heart. What's up with that? Who hardened Pharaoh's heart: Pharaoh or God? Apparently, they both did!

Not trying to ruin your day or cause you to lose your faith, but how can God—who is the defender of the oppressed—kill the firstborn children of Egypt? And if God doesn't change, and Jesus Christ is the same yesterday, today, and forever (Hebrews 13:8), and Jesus has always been God from the beginning of time, how do we reconcile God's retributive justice on wicked, oppressive Egypt (and their firstborn—yikes) with hippie Jesus giving peace signs in Luke?

I think the task of good Bible reading is noticing things you didn't see before. It's also letting the truth hold that incredible tension.

Ken Malmin, the dean of Portland Bible College, used to tell us in his Old Testament History course, "All truth is in tension." Ken likened it to a pup tent that has drawstrings pulling on either side of it to keep it up.

What if God is the perfect judge, and his judgment is always perfect, and he never goes too soft or too hard but always nails it right on the head? And what if God is loving, but he's also holy—two concepts that appear to be competing but work hand in hand.

And what if my sense of right and wrong and your sense of right and wrong are problematic because a) I'm not God, b) you're not God, c) that's really good, and d) God should be totally trusted because he's got a proven track record?

The coming Old Testament stories are full of paradox—none more than the exodus story. Pay attention to these major themes. Show interest as a reader in the story. Forget what you came to the text

needing or insisting upon today and get lost in the
story of salvation history.

MAKE A NOTE

_____

_____

_____

_____

_____

_____

_____

_____

_____

_____

_____

_____

_____

_____

_____

_____

If you're reading Leviticus trying to get a spiritual nudge from the Holy Spirit about whether or not to date that loser or buy that house, you're missing out big time. Because God is the star of Leviticus, and he begins to give us some huge ideas about himself, such as that he is a person—not an impersonal cosmic force—and he has preferences.

Israel is lucky to be in relationship with him. Five seconds ago they were quarrying stones and building pyramids at a 100% discount. Next minute, God destroys the entire Egyptian army with water in the same way he destroyed depraved humanity in the days of Noah. Israel did absolutely nothing except lay out a towel on the beach and let the surf do the hard work.

Israel doesn't serve a weak, lame, puny god like the gods of Egypt that were no match for YHWH. They serve the God of the universe who made everything. But they don't get to serve him however they want. And some of them are gonna have to find that out the hard way. They don't get to project onto or manipulate him.

God doesn't want his people to be anything like the other cultures. He wants his people to reflect the God they worship because you always become like what you worship. He wants them to be clean, and just, and fair, and merciful, and different—he wants them to be holy.

Holiness has to do with being set apart or different or morally clean or uncontaminated. Yhwh is a holy God, and he has a way of doing things. So he begins to tell Moses how the people of Israel must live and worship if they want him to stick around. Now, they'd be crazy to not have Yhwh as their God—he's the top gun—so they have to play ball. And that means unlearning and relearning ways of worship.

Notice all the details in worship? God has preferences. And this principle still applies today. Church isn't about me and my preferences, it's about God and his preferences.

Sadly, many of us have a misunderstanding of how grace works: we think that grace means we can worship God however we want. And that's just not the case. Grace means you didn't deserve to be in relationship with God—and you could never deserve to be in relationship with God—but because of the kindness and mercy of God, you who were once far away have been brought near (Ephesians 2:13). Now, as a result of the mercy of God, you find out what pleases him, and you give him that.

The heart of Old Testament worship and New Testament worship is the same. It isn't about me; it's about God. My heart is to know him—what pleases him—and be empowered by his grace to serve him.

Even when I don't get or agree with his preferences.

Reading Leviticus is a lesson in humility. It's an exercise in decentralizing yourself and putting God at the center, whose ways are totally not your ways. Leviticus 2:13 reads, "You shall season all your grain offerings with salt. ...with all your offerings you shall offer salt." Meaning, don't give God something you wouldn't even eat, and then expect that everything is good.

Reading the Law can be a challenge because it's like, "Do I or do I not get this tattoo? Am I not supposed to be eating bacon right now?"

The Mosaic laws in books like Leviticus could be roughly divided up into three parts: the moral law (moral directives that pass through the cross, and we know these because they are emphasized by Christ and the apostles), the ceremonial law (laws pertaining to the priesthood, tabernacle, and its operations), and the civil law (laws having to do with the nation of Israel).

"No tats" and "don't eat bacon" are national prohibitions that seem to be lifted for the most part in the book of Acts as the Holy Spirit is poured out on the Gentiles. The ceremonial laws about the sacrifices and altars are fulfilled in the person and work of Christ. The moral laws like "don't murder" and "don't have sex with animals" are keepers.

YHWH had his hands full trying to get Israel to be their own nation, and unlike all the other nations whose culture (day-to-day life) was downstream from their cults. So things like tattoos for these ancient peoples were deeply spiritual. YHWH didn't want Israel to be like anybody else: not in dress, in diet, or in law. They were to be unique, almost like a prophetic sign. They were supposed to stick out like a sore thumb.

Rather than getting lost in Leviticus, trying to parse out which rules are for you or why God would ban delicious bacon, it's probably better to read a little in reverse, knowing that God is actually cool with bacon (Acts 10:15), and that there was a danger of Israel absorbing spiritual practices from surrounding people groups who worshiped idols.

God was asking Israel to surrender their whole life to him and trust that this new way of life would be a form of worship to him, as well as protect them from the idolatry of other nations. For example, drinking blood was how people in the ancient Near East believed you could get power. God didn't want them to look to animals for power, but rather to him, so he forbids it.

And consider how Romans 12:1-2 may look for you. Offering your whole life to God is a reasonable act of worship, seeing as he has set you free from slavery and bondage to sin, and that getting caught up in the new community of faith we call the Church, with its culture of marriage, giving, fellowship, and prayer will keep you from places you ought not to be! Half of spiritual warfare is being in the right place at the right time!

MAKE A NOTE

_____

_____

_____

_____

_____

_____

_____

_____

_____

_____

_____

_____

_____

_____

After setting the nation of Israel up for worship, Moses begins to prepare them for warfare; the men available for battle are counted, the division of allotments in the promised land are made, and further assigning of various roles and duties in the nation are completed. But as Moses begins to move the nation out of the Sinai Peninsula toward the Jordan, the wheels start to come off the buggy.

Rebellion and authority issues are a major theme in this book. Miriam and Aaron (Moses' sister and brother) take issue with a recent marriage choice of Moses, and God has to put them in their place. God says the most remarkable thing to them during the family conference: that he doesn't speak to Moses the way he speaks to other prophets—in riddles and dreams—but rather as a man speaks to his friend, face to face. Old Testament scholar Bruce Waltke suggests that this mirrors the delivery method of the New Testament: both the Old and New Testaments are established by "face-to-face revelation."[4]

The point here is to underscore the reliability of the covenant that YHWH has made with Israel and ultimately Israel's reception of that covenant. As you read these first five Books of Moses, remember that you are reading the Bible of the first Christians and the Bible of Jesus. These things were "written for our instruction" (Romans 15:4), and none more than the narrative we see in Numbers.

If we think of Numbers as a story about a church (well, it technically is—Stephen calls Israel the "congregation in the wilderness" in Acts 7:38), it starts to make a lot of sense. Moses is the lead pastor and sees the spiritual direction the church needs to move in; he sees the ground that needs to be taken. And ten spies who whip themselves into a state of anxiety-induced paranoia and catastrophization start lying to the congregation about the obstacles they saw in the promised land ("the land devours its inhabitants!").

God smokes the ten spies, but then this creates a larger showdown with the power brokers and financiers of the fear: the tribal leaders. And God smokes them too.

The bodies start to pile high.

Moses lets his anger get the best of him. And God tells Moses that the entire congregation will wander in the wilderness and die of unbelief.

So what are we looking for in the book of Numbers? We are looking for patterns of unbelief in our own hearts.

This is one of the scariest narratives for me, personally, because of how many people I've seen choose unbelief and the corresponding life of wilderness wandering, never coming to the place that God had for them, all because they had a ton of rebellion operating inside of them.

I'm a rebellious guy by nature, and as much as I get so angry at the children of Israel in this narrative, I can't help but think I'd be caught up in the grumbling and complaining against Pastor Moses.

When God wants to take us to the next level, he doesn't send us Ozempic: he sends us a personal trainer. And personal trainers suck. They make you do stuff you don't wanna do. But sane people accomplish insane things with a trainer because a) they recognize their need, b) they show humility in submitting themselves to the harsh tutelage of the trainer, and c) they trust the trainer even in their discomfort.

Perhaps the lesson is that some things in us need to die off before we are ready for seasons of victory in God (pride, old aspirations for our life, ungodly metrics, unbiblical ways of thinking). And new generations of faith need to be released in us (desperation for more of God, wisdom to learn from the past, and willingness to trust the Lord with all our heart), so we can be led by the Spirit into the promised land—a land that he thought of in the first place, and a land of optimal human flourishing for us.

MAKE A NOTE

NUMBERS 32
↓
DEUTERONOMY 32

The most common interaction I have with readers of Deuteronomy is, "I can't believe how kind and loving and merciful the God of the Old Testament is!" And that's what I think will catch you by surprise as you read today.

We often come into our readings of the Old Testament a little confused, thinking that Old Testament God is bad cop, and New Testament God is good cop. You're at the police station because you sinned, and the Father comes in and clobbers you across the face with a phone book while screaming at you. Jesus barges in and yanks the red-faced Father off you (to your relief), closes the interview room door, and offers you a cigarette.

You're trembling, deeply inhaling a Marlboro Light nervously, pointing at the Father whose face is pressed against the interview glass door, begging Jesus, "Save me from that guy!"

Comical as it is, that's what some of us believe about the God of the Old Testament, and what ends up happening is we come to the text with a bias that blinds us from seeing the reality, which is the absolute opposite of that.

First, Jesus is Yʜᴡʜ; Jesus has always been God and always will be. He was Yʜᴡʜ at the burning bush, Yʜᴡʜ who led the armies of God, and Yʜᴡʜ who made a covenant with Abraham.

Second, Jesus bases all his teaching from these words given to Moses by (you guessed it) himself.

Keeping these simple ideas in mind, consider this: the type of Judaism that exists during the time of Jesus and the apostles was quite different to what we read in Deuteronomy, perhaps a result of national zeal stemming from the embarrassment suffered by the post-exilic community.

Let me explain: imagine coming back to Israel after seventy years in Babylonian captivity, determined to never again transgress the Law of God because you don't wanna get kicked out of God's land again!

Problematically, this well-intentioned zeal took on too many dos and don'ts that had no precedent in Moses. In order to not get close to the edge of the cliff, the Pharisees would create ten safety precautions and guard rails that eventually became more important than the Law of God itself!

We could summarize the Judaism of the Pharisees as red tape—rules and regulations that Moses had never even imagined. The irony was that all these additional prohibitions didn't change anyone's hearts, and that's what God was after the whole time.

The New Testament critiques the legalistic, added-to, burdensome brand of Judaism proffered by the Pharisees, and rightly so. But as you read Deuteronomy, you see a pure type of Judaism that Jesus himself whole-heartedly participated in—one that promotes relationship with God and a heart that loves the Lord and adheres to laws that promote and safeguard optimal human flourishing.

The Pharisees over-emphasized externals, but the Law of God emphasized the internal spiritual state.

Don't believe me yet? Read Deuteronomy. Some theologians have called this book (Second Law) the "Book of Grace."[5]

Deuteronomy 10:16 famously reads, "Circumcise therefore the foreskin of your heart, and be no longer stubborn." Paul the Apostle will pick up on this in his letter to the Romans, explaining that this is what righteousness is all about—the heart.

Later in Deuteronomy 30:6, Moses predicts, "And the Lord your God will circumcise your heart and the heart of your offspring, so that you will love the Lord your God with all your heart and with all your soul, that you may live."

You seeing this yet?

This is what Jesus and the apostles are talking about, and what is ultimately accomplished by the work of the Holy Spirit who indwells us. God himself helps us to love him by putting his mark on the most intimate part of our souls, cutting away the flesh and giving us the ability to love him with every part of us.

MAKE A NOTE

DEUTERONOMY 33
⬇
JUDGES 9

Moses has gotten the people of Israel ready for the Canaanite conquest. They are at the edge of the Jordan River about to cross over and take the promised land.

This new generation eagerly desires to differentiate itself from the rebellious generation that grumbled, complained, rejected God's leadership, and mutinied against YHWH himself. As you read Joshua, note how careful to obey the Law of Moses this generation is— they do not play!

Consider the Achan narrative (perhaps the only place in the entire book where failures happen), and his seemingly minor disobedience is treated like a plague by both God and the people. Perhaps you read his story and feel like Joshua and the people's dealing with him and his family is overreactive—you are correct. But consider the position they are in: they are outnumbered and outgunned in Canaan. Without God's help, they are totally done. And they've fully committed: they just destroyed Jericho, and now all the inhabitants of Canaan will band together against these foreign invaders.

It's too late to back out.

And the defeat at Ai (and the casualties they suffer) is a painful reminder that without God's intervention their goose is cooked. Israel cannot perform hard enough to win the promised land. The only ace-up-the-sleeve they have is total obedience to the Law of Moses: this is how they will have "good success," as outlined in Joshua 2.

Reading the Canaanite conquest and Achan narrative tragedy from your modern position is probably going to create more questions than answers: Why does God devote the Canaanite men, women, children, and animals to destruction? Why does Achan's entire family have to perish? Even the Law of Moses tells us that a son will not die for the sins of the father, and a father will not die for the sins of the son (Deuteronomy 24:16); Ezekiel re-affirms God's commitment to this (Ezekiel 18:20). So what gives?

With respect to the Canaanite conquest, here are two things to consider: firstly, these people were extremely evil and practiced child sacrifice, among many other abominations; secondly, Dr. Michael Heiser has suggested that it is possible that the mass genocide of the Canaanites was God's way of destroying the Nephilim bloodline.[6] That would mean that God is trying to rid the earth of people that are half-angel and half-human: an attempt to subvert God's good plans for humanity. Essentially, these people could have been monsters, hence why the spies referred to all of them as giants (Numbers 13:32-33).

It's important to note that nowhere in the Old Testament does God instruct Israel to totally wipe people out—not the Egyptians, not the Assyrians, not the Babylonians—only the Canaanites are deemed worthy of total annihilation.

With respect to the Achan narrative, it is probable that Achan's family were complicit in his robbing of God's stuff. God expressly told Joshua that Jericho would be his. It was to serve as a burnt sacrifice to God: a first-fruits offering. The people really needed the stores and goods and livestock and wealth of Jericho, but God wanted a) total loyalty and b) the first best thing.

If they really believed God would give them the rest of the land, dedicating Jericho to destruction was an incredible act of faith. Stealing from Jericho was an act of disbelief in God, that he wouldn't provide over and above what the people needed. In addition, the walls of Jericho fell down! God himself took that city, and word spread throughout the entire Canaanite peoples that Israel had a mighty God. Yhwh was getting glory for himself over the weak and pathetic Canaanite deities.

We should assume that Achan's adult family were guilty before the Lord and not innocent because God is not a God who kills the innocent. The narrative also mirrors the faith of Rahab the harlot whose entire family is saved by faith.

Achan is a son of Israel, but his act of rebellion against God (that's what unbelief is) infects his family, who take part in his treachery, and they are all destroyed. Rahab is a prostitute and a Canaanite woman, but her act of faith in Yhwh infects her family, who take part in her faith with God and his people, and they are all saved and added to Israel.

Achan is an insider who is made an outsider because of unbelief; Rahab is an outsider who is made an insider because of faith. In fact, Rahab marries into Israel, and she is in the genealogy of David and Jesus. Jesus is proud to have a former prostitute in his family tree—a woman who believed God and was made righteous!

MAKE A NOTE

_____

_____

_____

_____

_____

_____

_____

_____

_____

_____

_____

JUDGES 10
↓
1 SAMUEL 22

This is some of the most exciting historical and theological reading of the entire Bible, following the story of Israel's transition from a theocracy to a monarchy.

The time of the Judges proves chaotic: there is no clear leader, the tribes are fractured and suffer as a result, and a cycle of spiritual rebellion, oppression, and cries for help continue throughout the book. But before we move into the time of the kings, the backstory of Israel's greatest king is introduced in the book of Ruth.

Ruth is a Moabite, the result of incest (Genesis 19:37-38) from the story of Lot and his daughters. The Moabites are idolators and raiders (as we see from the book of Judges) with a sketchy bloodline, not the type of people Israel would want to get friendly with. But there's a famine in the land, and a certain

Israelite family sojourns to Moab for survival. His sons take Moabite wives while they are there, but all the men die, leaving the Moabite widows and Naomi the Israelite helpless.

Ruth the Moabite travels back to Israel with Naomi in order to take care of her mother-in-law: an act of kindness that is totally unusual. In telling Naomi that her God will become Ruth's God, Ruth is indicating that she means to stay in Israel indefinitely. Back in the ancient Near East, people worshiped the gods of the land in which they dwelled, and deities were the very rulers and guardians of specific geographical locations. This is why Naaman the Syrian leper will take dirt from Israel back to his native land. It is insinuated that he will spread the Israeli dirt around the corners of his house, thereby invoking the power of the God of that land over his home, saying, "My house belongs to Yhwh, the God of Israel who saved me."[7]

Ruth ends up marrying Boaz, a wealthy distant relative of Naomi's, and her great-grandson will be David, King of Israel. David is not ashamed to have Ruth the Moabite as his ancestor, and neither is Jesus.

This story would have been recorded by the Davidic dynasty authors, who find David's checkered past endearing. David's life is marked by incredible humility, and that's why Israel loves him. His bloodline is just as flawed as he is, but the people somehow love him for it. It's a paradoxical take on leadership, particularly when it's juxtaposed to the story of Saul, the first king of Israel, who has all the right angles but none of the heart.

Samuel the prophet's backstory is also wild. Samuel and David's lives are introduced to us through the women of faith and courage that brought them into the world. We know nothing about Saul's mother, and everything about Ruth and Hannah: two women who suffered deeply.

It's important to see God's kindness and love toward the seemingly insignificant in these passages. This is an agrarian society. Men had higher perceived functional value, and women were merely expected to reproduce and child-rear. Ruth and Hannah find themselves helpless and powerless, one without a husband and another without a child. God sees them, leads them, visits them, and performs wonders through them.

MAKE A NOTE

1 SAMUEL 23
↓
1 KINGS 1

There's a popular family drama about a wealthy aging patriarch with four competitive and dysfunctional children who do not possess the wherewithal to lead the family business well. They are cutthroat, backstabbing, vindictive, and anxious, and they are all vying for their father's attention.

This is the original succession story.

David is the greatest king who ever lived: greater than Solomon because David's successes didn't lead him away from the Lord. Even when David sins, he returns to the Lord with his whole heart. For all of Solomon's wisdom, wealth, and wives, he cannot find his way back to the source of the family power—YHWH.

David's secret is a heart after God that is daily rekindled in worship and devotion. Solomon has a heart that is studied in the ways of God but ultimately becomes disloyal.

The tragedy of the passages you are about to read is how David fails to be a father. This is a repeated theme in this literature. Eli the priest fails to father; Samuel the prophet fails to father; David the king fails to father. The priest, prophet, and king form the three-fold cord of Israel's spiritual and governmental life, and they are all seen as incapable of replicating devotion for the things of God in the next generation. The good starts of Saul and Solomon form an inclusio for the kingship of David. It's not enough to begin well; it's about finishing well and passing on the legacy of faith.

David loves his kids more than his own life, but his inability to confront and correct (or give tough love) backfires. His own son Absolom attempts patricide, partly because David refuses to deal with Amnon.

What we will hopefully see in these stories of Saul, David, conquests, family, and Solomon are insights into our own lives. God uses incredibly flawed people, and if he only used perfect people, he wouldn't use anyone.

Yet these things are written for our learning. What can we glean from them? What is God saying to us through these stories? What are the prophetic warnings in the book for us today? What areas in our life is the Holy Spirit gently reminding us to pay attention to?

As you read this action-packed, drama-filled history, allow the story to read you this time.

Family life appears to be the spiritual breaking point for the nation; a chain is only as strong as its weakest link. And while the monarchy is expected to be powerful and courageous and wise and good, the little foxes that spoil the vine need paying attention to. All that strength and wealth and wisdom is laid waste in a generation because a mighty warrior couldn't be a dad.

The bucolic harpist, the giant-slaying patriot, the kingdom-uniting regent, the scripture-writing poet—these memorable archetypes all fade to black as the inability to foster spiritual vitality comes to the foreground.

MAKE A NOTE

Solomon begins to reign in Israel and the nation achieves incredible civic and royal feats. Solomon has more wealth than Elon Musk and solidifies treaties and cooperation with his neighbors. Israel is safe under his watch because the Lord is with Solomon for most of his life.

But something shifts in 1 Kings 7. Work on the house of the Lord is paused for thirteen years as Solomon builds his own house and a house for the daughter of the pharaoh. God's house comes after Solomon's and the pagan sidepiece's. That's the shift in the narrative, and the building of the temple is the inclusio for this section: to show us that spiritual confusion is stirring in Solomon that wasn't there before.

Solomon's wisdom begins to totally disappear and becomes unhitched from the Law of Moses. What was once his strength now becomes a double weakness. The Law of Moses specifically tells the kings of Israel not to multiply wives and horses. Kings back in the day would have many wives so that they would have many alliances. The children born to these women would be a living testament to a kind of duality: two cultures in one. The problem was that these foreign wives brought their foreign gods—something they should not have done, seeing that Yhwh was the God of the land. Rather than adapting to the religion and culture of Israel, Solomon turned a blind eye to their idolatry because he fell in love with them.

He had his father's problem: no tough love.

The women began to turn Solomon's heart toward their foreign gods. Soon enough, the capital city had shrines and Asherahs to all kinds of deities. God was incredibly upset, but because of the faithfulness of David, he was patient.

Solomon also multiplied horses (built his army up) in the common parlance. But God didn't want the kings of Israel to have false hope or a sense of security that came from self. Yhwh had given them the land. He was the one who cleared out all the Canaanite tribes—seven nations larger and stronger than they! YHWH delivered them during the time of the judges; he was the one who anointed David and strengthened the kingdom. But now that Solomon was rich and felt a sense of determination and self-reliance as a result of the great wisdom he had (that God had given him!), he started making bonehead decisions.

As we read on through 1 Kings, things begin to unravel quickly. Solomon's son is a moron (of course), and the northern tribes revolt under Jeroboam, who creates a golden calf resembling the one that Aaron constructed at the foot of Sinai. The ten northern tribes amalgamate as Israel, and the two southern tribes amalgamate as Judah and stay loyal to Solomon's son, Rehoboam.

As you read on through this section, keep in mind that there are two kingdoms now: the northern nation of Israel (an idolatrous, deeply corrupt state) and the southern kingdom of Judah (the line of David, an idolatrous state that sometimes sees revival).

God in his mercy raises up two incredible prophets during this time in Israel and Judah's history: Elijah and Elisha. They will primarily minister to the backslidden nation of Israel because YHWH is jealous for his people and continually calls them to repentance.

One of the wicked kings of Israel, Ahab, marries a woman named Jezebel, a Phoenician princess, who brings her fertility god to Israel in an effort to produce economic prosperity like that of the Phoenicians, who were allies of Ahab and who were filthy rich. The fertility gods were the ones responsible to make it rain. Well, YHWH decides it won't rain in order to prove a point: Jezebel and her god have no business being in Israel. Israel was YHWH's territory, and YHWH won't be showed up by these loser gods.

The famine is so severe throughout the land that people are dropping like flies. But God shows his kindness to a widow and her son, who provide for the prophet even at the risk of their own lives. YHWH is so amazed at this story that Jesus will bring it up during his ministry.

Be careful to note that while God is doing battle with foreign gods and trying to reconcile nations to himself, he takes care of his prophet and a foreign widow who is suffering. Or note the humility that Naaman the leper, a full-on Syrian general, shows when his wife and female servant boss him around, telling him to go to Israel to see a prophet for his healing.

God is so attracted to people who humble themselves before him.

These stories are meant to stir our faith and expectation toward God today: a God who knows our needs even before we ask, and who looks for opportunities to show himself strong to those who will put their hand up for help.

MAKE A NOTE

_____

_____

_____

_____

_____

_____

_____

_____

_____

_____

Today we will read about the last of the kings of Israel and Judah. The Assyrian Empire overwhelms and essentially carries into oblivion the northern kingdom of Israel, but it is halted at the gates of Jerusalem in their attempt to overthrow the southern kingdom of Judah. And this is because they insult Yhwh in the process.

Hezekiah, the king of Judah, is encouraged by the prophet Isaiah to stand fast and see the deliverance of God. Hezekiah is a mostly good king who looks to Yhwh for help.

Josiah eventually reigns as king of Judah and is the most devout king since David. He reinstitutes the Levitical and temple system, restores the tabernacle of David with its loud and demonstrative worship, and rids the land of idols. His reforms and heart for God are unparalleled.

But after him will come kings who are wicked and evil, idolators who forsake Yhwh for other gods.

Here's an important thing to note, and I'm sure you've been noticing this along the way: the land belongs to Yhwh. It's his, and it was given to Israel on a lease. Think of the Law of Moses as the lease agreement, and Israel is now at the point where they have made an art of breaking the terms of the lease.

Yhwh promised in Deuteronomy—through the final words of Moses to the people—that he would kick them out of the land. The secret to possession of the promised land has always been and will always be maintaining a relationship with Yhwh. He isn't looking for perfection: that's why the sacrificial system exists. He is anticipating failures. But he's not someone who flies off the handle when Israel transgresses the Law. He's lovingly made arrangements for renewal. Tragically, Israel refuses to be healed.

Having rejected Yhwh and violated the terms of the lease beyond repair, they will be kicked out of Yhwh's land for the exact number of years the land did not lay fallow, according to the Law of Moses.

These histories of Kings and Chronicles are extremely helpful in interpreting the ministry of the prophets: the kind of cyclical idolatry and overall stupidity they were addressing during their tenure as the oracle of God.

In the reading today, you'll see the ministry of Isaiah very clearly. As you begin to get into the other prophetic voices, identifying the time period and corresponding rulers will help frame a helpful backdrop.

As you enter the book of Chronicles, you might be thinking, *Didn't I just read this?* While there are some significant narrative overlaps, these books are written from two different perspectives. Samuel and Kings were written before the exile, Chronicles was written after the exile, and this means that there are two different messages for two different audiences. The audience of Samuel and Kings is being warned to obey God and pay attention to the Law; the audience of Chronicles needs hope that God will renew and restore his people.

Chronicles focuses on the lives of David and Solomon, the southern kingdom of Judah, and the theme of restoration.

As you read today, watch for the encouragements in Kings to pay attention to the secret of promised-land success. And as you begin Chronicles, let what God did in the past fill your soul with hope for what God will do in the future. He's the same God—yesterday, today, and forever!

MAKE A NOTE

_____

_____

_____

_____

_____

_____

_____

_____

_____

_____

_____

_____

1 CHRONICLES 21
⬇
2 CHRONICLES 33

The cycles of the books of Judges, Kings, and Chronicles form an inclusio to the story of David (Israel's greatest king), who sought the Lord with all his heart and kept Yнwн at the absolute center of Israel's spiritual and governmental life.

In Judges, we see the repeated theme that there was no king in Israel, and everyone did what was right in their own eyes. The cycle of personal preferences, oppression, and cries for help at the atomic level of Israeli national life are repeated by the very kings of Israel who were meant to insulate Israel from this kind of thing.

What are we meant to do as we read the stories of the kings in the chronicles of Judah? Well, the kings are to be compared to David—the authors even do that for us (2 Chronicles 34:2; 1 Kings 3:14; 2 Kings 22:2).

David is the penultimate king who prioritizes the Law of God and the presence of God simultaneously. In John 4:23, Jesus tells us that God is looking for worshipers who will worship him in spirit and truth. David created an atmosphere in Israel where the Law of God was not just kept, but also cherished as the golden key that brought God's life-giving presence into the spiritual and governmental life of the nation.

The Law wasn't seen as something to be tolerated, but rather as the reasonable rider of a desired celebrity. David was smitten. He had tasted and seen that Yhwh was his shepherd and the lover of his soul. But it was more than a skin-deep affair. David went out of his way to look into the Law of Moses to find out what God loved.

It's like doing a forensic deep-dive into the likes and dislikes of someone you love; you discover what their preferences are—what makes them tick—and then you buy the tickets for the show they always wanted to see, or you take them to the town in Italy where their grandparents were married. You have paid attention to the details of their communication, and you've shown them how much you love them by bringing precision to your adoration.

Abel offered God the first of his flock and the fatty portion (what was costly and precious to him); Cain offered some fruit (an offering that he didn't care about because it didn't cost him). In the Old Testament, Moses had to tell people not to offer lame sacrifices—animals that had been maimed or were essentially impossible to sell or use for good meat. God was saying, "That's what you think of me? You'd give me something that you despise yourself?"

David was the most romantic worshipper ever. He saw the Law of Moses as God's history (rightly so) and set himself to know God on a forensic level so as to give him offerings that pleased him. David even discovered some unique offerings (by the Spirit) himself (Psalm 141:1-2), things that God was ultimately after.

David set a precedent that Yhwh wasn't like the other gods. We will see this throughout David's literature in the psalms. Yhwh was not a god made of wood; he was a living, breathing, life-giving person who knows all, and sees all, and is worthy of all glory.

The kings of Israel and Judah kicked Yhwh out of their hearts long before they kicked him out of his own temple. They refused to set themselves to seek the Lord.

Now, some of you may have a bone or two to pick with David. He was a murderer and an adulterer, and yet he was called "a man after God's own heart" in 1 Samuel 13:14. How do we reconcile this? Spirit-and-truth worship isn't about perfection; it's about repentance.

Most of us will never murder someone or cheat on our spouse, yet many of us live in an unrepentant and idolatrous manner. We have a relationship with God on our terms, where we presume to love and worship him in a manner that suits us. And we expect God to regard our offering, not understanding that God will have no regard for the offering of Cain.

If you want to love God, you have to read the Book, find out what he loves, and give him what he desires. And if you violate the Book, you have to admit that you are wrong, and that God is right.

Spirit-and-truth worship is a tension many of us are unwilling to live in because we think that life is all about our preferences, modes, desires, temperament, and way of thinking. We regularly put the Bible on trial, and in doing so, put the God of the Bible on trial. That's the way of the kings of Israel and the people in the book of Judges: they did what was right in their own eyes without inquiring of the Lord by way of his Word.

The key of David—the secret of possessing the inheritance that God has for you—is a repentant and humble heart that decides God is right all the time, his Word is right all the time, he is worth following, worth sacrificing everything good in your life for, worthy of your attention and devotion and allegiance, and someone whose presence is make-or-break in your life.

David's personal and corporate routines of worship, as we will see in Psalms, were instituted as protective hedges over and against outside influences that would seek to steal his affections and attentions for Yhwh.

It's important to note that only when David's tabernacle was reinstated (the mass gathering of corporate worship accompanied by songs of praise), were the kings in revival. Where there was no worship, there was no obedience to Yhwh, and devastation was just around the corner.

Worship became the catalyst for law keeping in the Davidic tradition. A heart that loved the Lord obeyed his Word, and when the Law was obeyed, the kingdom was secure.

MAKE A NOTE

2 CHRONICLES 34

⬇

JOB 5

Where I live in Tennessee, we get tornado warnings fairly often. My wife is from Australia and I'm from Canada, so we aren't used to tornado watches every other month. My wife specifically gets pretty antsy; she follows these tornado nerds that have a makeshift weather channel/bunker from which they broadcast live whenever a storm cell moves into the area.

If you've ever seen the devastation that twisters bring, you'll know it's a little nerve-racking. Properties are literally unrecognizable: survivors stand outside their homes wondering where to start picking up the pieces.

As we come out of the story of the kings, we get right into the books of Ezra and Nehemiah. These guys are part of the rebuilding crew. They've just arrived at the scene of the tornado with the exilic community, and they are picking up the pieces of what used to be their homeland.

Israel has been in Babylonian captivity for seventy years, and now God is orchestrating political events so his people can come back and rebuild. Ezra is the spiritual architect of God's restoration project in Jerusalem, and Nehemiah is the political architect. Ezra and Nehemiah are both called by God and carry unique giftings, facing obstacles in the way of recovery.

Ezra is passionate about teaching the people the secret to possessing the land: adherence to the Law of Moses. The zeal that Jesus will encounter in the Pharisees comes from the painstaking work of Ezra in establishing a meticulous fervor in the people for the Law.

Nehemiah is the best book in the Bible on leadership. Nehemiah navigates the greatest empire in the world, taking chances and currying favor. He faces opposition from external and internal enemies; he battles discouragement that comes from total momentum loss. Nehemiah knows that his work is totally in the hands of God and learns to trust God's timing.

Ezra and Nehemiah's spiritual and governmental work are accompanied by the prophesying of Haggai and

Zechariah. Prophetic work is always for the purpose of building up (1 Corinthians 14:1-5), even if things need to be pulled down in order for new foundations to be laid.

The book of Esther follows Ezra and Nehemiah as a hopeful encouragement for the post-exilic community: a story that centers on God's powerful sovereign hand over the Jewish people. Why is God so invested in them? Why is the political history of a mono-racial ethno-state in our Bible? Doesn't God care about other people?

It's probably helpful to zoom out and answer that question at this point in our reading, so we can begin to put the pieces of the puzzle together. God is recording all this history so he can prove that he is faithful to his word.

In Genesis 3 when we fell, God immediately promised a seed that would crush the serpent's head. Jesus is the seed of the woman. But God has to make that seed full of meaning for us, and without a thematic drama, the seed has very little implication if introduced without any character development.

Everything you are reading—God's promises to Abraham, his deliverance of Israel out of Egyptian slavery, his revelation of his holiness, the concept of the promised land, the sacrificial system and the requirement of blood for sin, the advent of David and his revelation of worship, the cycles of judgment and deliverance, the failure of Israel as a nation to worship Yhwh, Babylonian exile and rebuilding—are all powerful archetypes of our spirituality.

We all go astray. We all seek our own way. But God is faithful to come after us. He reaches his hands out all day long. He will even be faithful to discipline us in order that we come to our senses and run back to him more dedicated than ever.

That's what happens to Israel.

God's covenants with Abraham and David involve the seed of the woman, the Messiah, coming through their lineage. So God is going to protect that lineage even when he disciplines it. Israel is lost in the Assyrian campaign, but Judah is protected even in Babylonian exile. Judah comes back. Yhwh documents Jesus' genealogy like a pedantic IRS auditor in order to prove that he kept his word.

Israel is the carrier of the promise, and that's why God will totally focus on them until the seed has come.

If God is able to work so providentially over the minutiae of hungry prophets or the large-scale chaos of war and empire, how much more is he able to take care of you? Maybe you feel like you're standing in the middle of a house that has been blown to smithereens, and you wonder if you'll ever be able to possess the hope or feel the momentum you once had. You can be reminded in today's reading that God's Word comes to give hope not just during the storm, but when you are standing in the hell of the aftermath of it.

MAKE A NOTE

I recently taught a class on theodicy: suffering, and why it happens. After examining six different theories of suffering with the students, my conclusion was that I don't know why suffering happens. None of the theories seem to really answer why trouble exists in our world the way it does.

Sometimes the Bible tells us why something happened to a specific person. When that happens, it's not a prescription for all suffering, it's a specific word from God on that particular case. Joseph suffered so Israel could be preserved.

In John 9:2, Jesus' disciples ask why a man was born blind. Did his parents sin? Did he? Jesus tells them that the man was born blind so that the works of God would be revealed. Then Jesus heals him.

Is that the case with all sickness? No, it's not.

Suffering isn't always redemptive: God wasn't trying to teach the Jews at Auschwitz a valuable life lesson. And it doesn't really seem to serve in such a way as to glorify God; although there are some who believe all suffering and even eternal damnation serve to glorify God.

And I suppose in a way—when we are all seated at the judgment seat of Christ—we will know better, and perhaps that is part of it. But in the here and now, we really don't know why suffering happens. All we know is that we are promised trouble by Jesus himself (John 16:33).

The book of Job is not about God prodding Job for genuine faith. Does God test the faith of people he loves? Yes (James 1:2-4). But is all suffering testing? Not necessarily. Does it all have a purpose? Perhaps not. Does all of it make one's life better? Hard to prove that the death of my friends' baby made the baby's life or theirs better.

Now, before you pour yourself a glass of wine and deconstruct your faith, consider this: Job is the oldest book in the Bible, and it asks the hardest questions about life. It actually gets better than that. The book of

Job isn't about Job being on trial, it's about God being on trial.

As long as humans have been sucking air on planet earth, they've been questioning the hand they've been dealt and why God would put them in this kind of position in the first place. So it's only fitting that the oldest book in the Bible deals with the hardest content: Why is life so messed up, and where is God in all of it?

Now, if you're the sort of person who presumes to think they have any kind of authority on how the world should work, or what fair actually is, or what justice ought to be, or exactly what kind of judgment should be passed down, you're gonna hate this book. Because in classic God form, it leaves us with more questions than answers.

First of all, there's a divine council of God's sons (administrative angels) who have just as many questions for God as we do. The stage of the book is set as one takes on an interlocutor or cross-examiner position, accusing God of coddling and protecting his most loyal subject, Job, in order to keep Job's faith alive. Satan (literally *adversary*, perhaps not "the devil," the singular personified character of evil as we understand him in the New Testament) tells God that humans won't love and trust him if things don't go their way, that their love is fickle, and that if hard times come, they'll turn their back on him just as fast as Lucifer and his fallen angels did.

God tells the prosecutor to have a field day; test Job, but don't kill him.

Taking advantage of God's invitation and ultimately manipulating the spirit of God's house rules, the angel goes off and kills Job's livestock and his family, and then—adding insult to injury—puts the grief-stricken Job in unbearable pain. Hilariously, he doesn't kill Job's wife. She must have been a piece of work. At some point she tells Job to "curse God and die" (Job 2:9).

Job is joined by three friends who all wax eloquent on the origin of evil and suffering. God essentially replies, "Were you there when I made the universe? Explaining myself to you is like you trying to explain to a worm how to make a sandwich."

Job holds to his conviction that God is trustworthy, and vindicates God, who is Job's redeemer. God doesn't have to do anything for Job, but he blesses him richly.

I don't know why bad things happen to good people or why good things happen to bad people, but I do know this: God is trustworthy.

Perhaps you've been tempted to try and force meaning on things that just won't perform under that kind of pressure. Maybe you've loaded way too much spiritual freight into good or bad circumstances, and you feel a bit phony, like you're living in a spiritual house of cards.

There is nothing retreatist or unintelligent about choosing to trust God no matter what happens in life. In fact, it's the exact choice the heroes of faith decided upon after working through the philosophical questions.

We don't know; God does. We aren't faithful; God is.

MAKE A NOTE

PSALM 19
⬇
PSALM 78

In every period of Israel's revival, there were songs. When the harp was hung upon the willow tree, there was oppression and spiritual bondage. David's harp playing had the ability to drive tormenting spirits away.

Here are two paradoxical statements about the psalms: isolating them from their musical context robs them of their spirit and potency. And on the other hand, the psalms should be prayed and memorized. I use three psalms for my daily liturgy (in this order): Psalm 23, Psalm 103, and Psalm 91.

So let's get a quick theology of Psalms and then a practical plan of usage for your reading today.

Regarding their theology, they are the spring from which all spiritual life in Israel flowed. They are the purest fountainhead—the secret sauce—of successful relationship with God. As you are noticing in your reading, YHWH always wanted our hearts, and the psalmist locks into this theme.

Here is a forty-thousand-foot-level overview of the nature of Psalms: while a lot of complaining, inquiring, petitioning, and general agonizing over sin or some other tragic circumstance goes on (the psalmists aren't afraid to tell God how they really feel), all of the psalms except one (the Black Psalm, Psalm 88) are accompanied by praise.

David gets something right that Job and the sons of Korah (who penned Psalm 88) don't: God will come through, so we can give him the praise in advance. You and I are stuck in the timeline, but God experiences all things at once because he stands outside of time. He sees the end from the beginning, like a boy holding a pencil and looking at both ends. David is prophetically inserting himself into the realm of God by petitioning and then praising God at the same time.

Perhaps you've thought that there's no right way to pray—I used to think that also. We would both be wrong. As our minds are renewed by the Spirit-inspired Scriptures, we are able to recognize that our attitude can be off. Should I be able to tell God anything? Well, God already knows everything. He's a heart reader, not a lip reader. But my heart needs some fixing. And as I read Scripture, my heart is cut into pieces under the conviction of the Holy Spirit. I recognize that I've been self-centered and not God-centered, that I actually have bitterness and lack faith, and that God deserves my honor and trust.

Getting practical now, I use the Scriptures like a paint-by-number, following the patterns that should orient my heart in verse and a posture that honors the Lord.

In the liturgical tradition (reciting, praying, or singing pre-written words), it is not considered inauthentic to sing something that may not be true at the time but is ultimately what one desires to feel or be. If I sing, "I love you, Lord," I may not feel like I love the Lord at all. Yet I sing it because I want it to be true. And a fact of life is that the heart and flesh can be stewarded. I sing the liturgy until I become the liturgy.

As you read Psalms, pray the psalms; and as you pray the psalms, ask the Lord that you become the psalms.

MAKE A NOTE

PSALM 79
⬇
PSALM 147

Learning the psalms as a pattern for prayer is quite easy to do; using them as a pattern for praise is the difficult thing—the intimidating, humiliating thing— but the very thing they were designed to accomplish. Note the emphasis on praise throughout these psalms, and once again consider that they were sung by a congregation.

Praise is the thing that God delights in. Psalm 22:3 suggests that YHWH is "enthroned" on the praises of his people. He sits down and rules in that place. He takes a posture of active authority in the atmosphere of praise.

Praise isn't something you can do in your heart only, just like love isn't something that remains a detached metaphysic subtlety.

There's a fascinating paradox in our Christian bone-to-pick with the secular term "make love": a term we've come to despise because of how it collapses a multidimensional reality into a singular act of lust. Yet it has its proper uses; love certainly needs to be made toward the object of its affection. What I mean is this: nobody who loves anybody can stop their love from seeping out of their soul and into their body. Love is incarnated and put on display in a physicality. This is Jesus' entire point when he explains "greater love" in John 15:13.

God demonstrates his love (Romans 5:8), and we ought to as well. Someone once said you can give without loving, but you cannot love without giving.

Praise as described in the Psaltery—clapping of the hands, singing, shouting, rejoicing (literally spinning around), dancing, lifting hands, congregational chanting—is a demonstrative adoration accompanied by music. This is what God loves. This is his love language—a fully embodied offering of love—that attracts his presence and glory.

And the truth is that all of us engage in these types of actions external to the congregational offering in some form throughout our lives. Look at the reserved and socially brittle English at their soccer games, who transform into flag-waving hippies at the sound and sight of their beloved team's anthem as they take the pitch. Consider our celebration at weddings, or what kind of grotesque joy would overtake us at winning the billion-dollar Powerball. God sees this and says, "I love it when you do that, and I want you to do that toward me. Show me that the revelation of my salvation and goodness and mercy and kindness and patience toward you has been internalized, that the gospel has truly been received."

Are we idolators? Will we dance at a concert but not for God? There's nothing wrong with dancing at a concert as long as the Lord isn't shortchanged. Or consider our credit card statement: Do we always have money for the things we love but never for God? Show me your credit card statement, and I'll show you your god.

Is there something you do that, when you do it, you lose track of time solely because you love it so much? That's playing Fortnite for me. I could play video games 'til my eyes bleed. But what time does the Lord get? Am I an idolator who offers the Lord lame sacrifices? The children of Israel used to bring God animals that they didn't even want, and God was rightly disgusted.

Praise (spiritual verse accompanied by music and physical demonstration) is not pentecostal, charismatic, Black, American, Australian, or modern. It's biblical.

And if it's in the Bible and it makes God happy, I'm going to give it to him because I love him and I want him to know it. My will must be conformed to his will. My body will obey the Lord; my soul will rejoice in the Lord. I will train my soul (my mind, will, and emotions) to magnify the Lord. I will remind myself—like David does—of the benefits of being in relationship with Yhwh (Psalm 103:1-5), and I will husband my life like a gardener husbands an unruly yard.

The psalms then become a training ground for the soul. They are where the sinner goes to be trained in righteousness.

Fasten the rebellious shoots of your heart to the tree-brace of Scripture, exactly as the psalmist is doing himself as he writes. Don't be led by your feelings but lead your feelings with the Word of God!

"Let everything that has breath praise the Lord!"[8]

MAKE A NOTE

PSALM 148
⬇
ECCLESIASTES 12

Have you ever been confused by the Bible? Get ready to scratch your head in today's reading. Proverbs and Ecclesiastes are full of paradoxes. Here's an example.

Proverbs 26:4 (NIV): "Do not answer a fool according to his folly, or you yourself will be just like him."

Ok. If someone is being an idiot, I shouldn't jump in and wrestle a pig. Good point. Next verse.

Proverbs 26:5 (NIV): "Answer a fool according to his folly, or he will be wise in his own eyes."

What? Now you want me to say something so this moron doesn't think he's right? Which one do I listen to? Both. And discernment will tell you in which context to apply which tool.

That's some top-of-the-Maslow-pyramid intelligence right there.

As we read through this ancient wisdom, we have to consider a couple things in our attempts to navigate it.

First, this stuff is made to be memorable, not necessarily perfectly theoretical.[9] It doesn't mean these things aren't true, it just means they are poetry first like, "A stitch in time saves nine." A stitch doesn't save exactly nine other stitches, but it may save some!

Second, Proverbs needs to be considered within the context of the rest of Scripture. It is to be read as a collection of proverbs.[10] As illustrated above, these verses are better explained in their immediate contexts as well as the context of the rest of the wisdom of Scripture.

Third, the proverbs are principles, not promises. God wants you to know how life generally works out. "A generous person will prosper" (Proverbs 11:25 NIV) doesn't mean that every person on planet earth who is generous ends up being rich or prosperous. Poverty or hard times don't show partiality. It's a principle in life that generally works out, and certainly there is both a natural and spiritual dynamic to it.

Wisdom isn't knowing everything; it's the application of knowledge or the art of applying what you know.

And that's the big idea of the book of Proverbs: getting some major building blocks like the fear of the Lord and obedience to his Word will give you insights on how to live your life well.

The book of Ecclesiastes, amazingly written by the same author, doesn't have as much confidence or certainty as Proverbs. Ecclesiastes seems to be the later reflections of a very wealthy and burned-out cynic. The young cynic hates the world; the old cynic laughs at the world.

Here we have an older cynic who seems to be a bit cavalier in his quick dismissal of the meaning of life. But this voice is a needed voice—a seldom heard voice—the voice of someone who has tried everything and then reduces life down to a couple big ideas. Much of what we chase is, in fact, vanity.

Now, there's a difference between the wise old cynic and the Nihilist, who even sees wisdom itself as pointless. The Bible is not endorsing indifference; it's presenting the experience of a guy who kept nothing from himself and wisely surmises that serving God and enjoying work is about as peak as life can get.

Identifying the big things that give people joy can help us guard against idolatry.

So as we read Proverbs, let's be careful to avoid formulaic theology that tends to make us think we can insulate ourselves from life, and rather consider that having a strategy can be rewarding.

And as we read Ecclesiastes, let's leave the "Chet Baker Sings" album on the shelf and refuse to self-indulge our prone-to-lethargic indifference, and rather focus the whole of our energy on enjoying our Creator and the many graces he has given us to steward.

MAKE A NOTE

_____

_____

_____

_____

_____

_____

_____

_____

Reading ancient literature can be a bit confusing at times. We have grown up in a culture that has fairly fixed ideas of virtue, although the boundaries of everything seem to be changing rapidly.

Much of what we believe about relationships, however, is assumed; it's given to us by the culture in which we have been raised. Most of us in Western culture would agree that romance is an important piece in lasting, loving, committed relationships, particularly in marriage. But for most of human history, romance took a back seat even in ancient Israel.

Marriage tended to be more transactional and utilitarian. It's hard to believe that was God's design for it because Scripture is replete with language that suggests romantic love and rejoicing in that love in the bounds of marriage. Christ himself takes on the role of a husband to the Bride, his Church, whom he loves and lays his life down for.

Song of Solomon is included in the wisdom literature for several reasons: first, because it comes from Solomon, and second, because it is wise to pursue romance in marriage.

The church fathers read Song of Solomon as an allegory of Christ and the Church, but this was because they didn't like the sexual nature of the book. I'm not denying that the book can certainly take on that allegorical meaning, but perhaps by dismissing the raw sexuality in it, we rob the book of its contribution to marriage in a cultural setting where romance within marriage was something often pushed to the side.

If you look at the narrative arc of polygamy, for example, in the Old Testament, the constant motif is tragedy. The only patriarch we have in Scripture who has a fairytale love story is Isaac, and God is the one who sets the whole thing up wonderfully. The wisdom of the book, then, confronts the culture into which it was birthed, and instructs couples in the joy of the pursuit of romantic love between one man and one woman.

And we get right into the book of Isaiah next. Let's zoom out quickly: Judah is getting close to the end of God's patience. The prophet Isaiah is challenging the people of Judah to say yes to God and his way of possessing their inheritance, but they insist on saying yes to everybody except God. The result is judgment and loss of the promised land.

In Isaiah 65, God says, "His servants will be called by a different name, so that the one who blesses himself in the land will do so by the God whose name is Amen, and the one who swears an oath in the land will do so by the God whose name is Amen."[11] *Amen* means "yes" or "so be it."

God is saying his name is Yes.

Paul says in 2 Corinthians 1:19-20 that "…in him it is always Yes. For all the promises of God find their Yes in him." Paul is saying that *yes* describes God's faithfulness. If we say yes to God, God always says yes to us, and his yes is a more powerful yes than ours because it brings a tidal wave of goodness and mercy that has been in motion toward us for all of time.

When we say yes to God and stay faithful to him, we unlock his faithfulness, which is far more potent.

Jesus self-identifies as "Amen" in Revelation 3:14. He was the one who said yes to the Father and was a faithful witness his whole life. We are invited to be Amen people: people who say yes to God and stay faithful to him.

As you read Isaiah today, take note of God's unwavering love and desire to show kindness to people who are running in the opposite direction of his presence. And be careful to mark all the opportunities God is giving his rebellious people to amend their no to a yes. The God of the Old Testament is mercy motivated. That should encourage you in the grace of the Lord Jesus Christ today!

MAKE A NOTE

I made the mistake of asking my dad what heaven would be like when I was nine. He told me that it would be a worship service that would last forever, and he said it a little too passionately for my liking—as if he couldn't wait. The problem was I was nine, and worship services weren't exactly my cup of tea. And my dad was a worship leader at church, so I felt like he was trying to sell me something I just wasn't really buying at that moment.

I still remember the panic and anxiety that gripped my soul, like trying to wake up from a bad episode of sleep paralysis. It messed with me for a year or so. I remember thinking to myself, "I don't wanna die because then I'll end up in heaven."

The judgment of God is coming upon the kingdom of Judah. Their stewardship of the promised land is coming to an end because they haven't said yes to God. Isaiah will record words of hope and comfort for the exiled people who come to their senses in the pigpen of Babylonian captivity, as well as the post-exilic community who will return home to rebuild. And while there is an experience or earthly fulfillment of Yhwh's promises of renewal, there is also a day coming when the earth itself—all of creation, in fact—will be renewed.

This latter half of Isaiah gives the New Testament Church theological context for everything Jesus the Messiah will accomplish for Israel and then ultimately for the Church. The kingdom of Jesus on earth is the launch of God's renewal program, which is "now but not yet": a program that is rolled out in phases until Jesus returns for the whole reconstruction, or better yet, reboot.

The point is that eternity is going to be something familiar. We aren't naked angel babies flying around with harps; neither are we stuck in a golden city floating in space, locked in a worship concert. I'd rather not.

The picture Isaiah gives us is a new earth—we are back here on earth, but earth itself has been renewed—it's not all crusty and angry at us because of the curse of sin; rather, it's become much more alive and welcoming, a place for optimal human flourishing. And we are doing human stuff: creating and organizing and making beautiful God's creation.

As a young man in my 20s, I began to revisit the questions I asked my dad about eternity and found incredible joy and hope in Isaiah's vision of a new heavens and new earth: a theme repeated by Peter and John in their respective writings (Isaiah 65:17-19, 22; 2 Peter 3:10-13; Revelation 21:1-5). Part of me gets really excited about what God is going to roll out for us. And that's essential to Christian hope, having an idea of God's goodness and that it will be familiar yet far superior—like a long-awaited sequel to a book that you couldn't put down.

The last 15 chapters of Isaiah are perhaps the most significant. Think of how the early Church would be reading this in light of the gospel of Jesus Christ and note these themes that would help the hearers identify Jesus as God's Amen—God's Yes—the fulfillment of God's promise to do away with sin and corruption.

As you read today, ask the Holy Spirit to show you to what lengths he went to describe Jesus to the hearers of Isaiah, so they could hear and see Christ when he arrived just as he promised.

MAKE A NOTE

_____

_____

_____

_____

_____

_____

_____

_____

_____

_____

_____

_____

_____

When I worked at McDonald's (three years, baby), I was given the absolute worst jobs that an employee could get (because I joked too much in the kitchen— my managers either loved or hated me):

- Backwash (all the washing up at the end of the night before closing) – which I came to enjoy.

- Grill (making the meat) – standing in front of a hot grill is nuts.

- Cleaning the vats – absolutely brutal.

- Emptying the grease traps – hands down, worst job. It smells like crap, and you gotta deal with a contagion of bees and flies.

- Cleaning the play place – kids vomit, pee, and poop in the balls and on the slides. It's gross.

That's the prophet Jeremiah. He had the worst job of anyone who ever served God. Paul the Apostle was trying his best to replicate the suffering of the "weeping prophet" (Jeremiah) and probably never came close.

And it isn't just what was done to Jeremiah (beatings, torture, imprisonment, and eventually martyrdom in Egypt), but rather what he had to see with his own eyes: children being eaten by their parents, the rape and murder of pregnant women at the hands of Babylonian soldiers, and the bodies piled high in the streets. Jeremiah was basically too good at his job: being the mouthpiece of Yhwh to the people who rejected him.

Reading the book of Jeremiah is a bit of a downer. The content of the book rolls out in stages of judgment, disaster, danger, defeat, and death of the nation.[12] It's not the most encouraging literature, but what is profound is God's desire for his people to turn back to him. At every stage, God yearns for their repentance so he can rescue them. He never gives up warning them.

There are two ways to see this: God is vengeful and scary, or God is compassionate and long-suffering.

Imagine a lifeguard is watching the surf and sees Jaws approaching the swimmers. The lifeguard yells out repeatedly with a bullhorn, "Please come back to the beach! There's a shark in the water!" But the bathers reject his advice and swim toward open water.

The lifeguard cries out again, but this time from his watchtower hooked up to a loudspeaker, "Please come back to the shore; there's a great white shark heading your way!" The swimmers are drunk, laughing at the lifeguard, and they start making fun of him.

Finally, the lifeguard runs out into the water with a dingy and outboard motor, speeds over the waves toward the drifting swimmers, and within feet of the morons, yells, "Here! Grab my hand! I can see the shark coming toward you! Get in the boat with me!"

But they start splashing water at him and call him a Karen.

Then Jaws eats them for lunch.

Was the lifeguard not compassionate?

The warnings of Jeremiah the prophet are the warnings of a God who loves life and desires to preserve it, not the yammerings of a vindictive megalomaniac with control issues who has a penchant for annihilation.

Context really matters.

Because we have just read the context of a God who delivers, loves, and desires to be with his people, yet at the same time desires covenant loyalty and loathes what idolatry does to the human body and soul, we can see that these warnings are just.

God is just; his justice is perfect.

So as we read Jeremiah, let us take note of the kindness and forbearance of God. And let's also be inspired by Jeremiah, a guy whose yes to God meant being the bad guy. Faithfulness to God for Jeremiah meant being hated by the people he was trying to warn.

Can we be faithful lifeguards to those God is desiring to save?

MAKE A NOTE

One of my favorite characters in Harry Potter (I get it, I'm going to hell for reading Harry Potter) is Draco Malfoy, the spoiled rich kid who plays the student antagonist throughout the series. Draco oozes with pride that stems from 1) his father's governmental position in the ministry of magic, 2) the purity of his wizard-family blood, 3) the student house into which he was sorted, and 4) his family's wealth. These four pillars hold up the temple of self-worship that Draco has erected to himself.

Now Draco is also always a small blunder away from an anxious crash: he's deeply insecure and desires the respect of his peers and the love of his father. As Draco's humanity becomes clear in the series, he becomes a little endearing—he's not as evil as he wishes us to think—and we are given a small window to see some virtue that his vices attempt to disguise.

Ezekiel is a true seer. He's from a priestly family and understands the whole game. He's like a pastor's kid who sees past all the spiritual facades into the very heart of the matter. Every prophet has a personal paradigm—a history or family trade—that makes up a map of meaning for the world. Sometimes I wonder if Jeremiah was a frat boy because when God calls him, he makes it super easy.

"Hey God, I don't know if I'm gonna be good at being a prophet."

"Bro, if I've called you, I'm gonna help you."

"Ok."

"Do you see that boiling cauldron?"

"Um, the one on the fire?"

"Yes, that one."

"Yeah, what about it?"

"My anger is boiling and that's what I'm gonna dump on Jerusalem."

"Oh dang! You are really speaking my language."

"Yes, I am. This is prophecy for dummies. Now let's have fun with a prophecy about almonds."

God would just point and rhyme for Jeremiah.

With Ezekiel, because of his background, he's got all this language and insight. His knowledge of the Levitical system is going to be a prophetic playground for the Holy Spirit to download wild stuff into his imagination.

Ezekiel sees four foundations for Judah's pride, kind of like Draco Malfoy's pride:

- pride of the gift of the land of Canaan that came in an eternal oath,

- pride of the covenant with Yhwh that came in an eternal oath,

- pride of Zion where God makes an oath to dwell forever, and

- pride of the Davidic covenant, an oath that rulers of the line of David will sit upon the throne forever.[13]

Judah thinks they can just act the fool and then hide behind Daddy's oaths to them.

And what Judah is about to find out about eternal oaths is that they go both ways. In the words of Daniel Block, "If Judah will be destroyed—and she will—it will not happen because Yнwн has reneged on his covenant commitment… he will abandon his temple and send his people into exile in a foreign land because the people of Israel have been unfaithful to him. This covenantal treachery demanded the rupturing of the deity-nation-land relationships."[14]

God never abandons his covenant; he was faithful. It was Israel that failed to be faithful. What we have to see in God's clipping of the house of David's political wings and rejection of his temple is that he is being faithful to his Word: he said he would do this if the children of Israel were unfaithful to him. We see this in Deuteronomy 28:15-68. It's right there in the Law of Moses, recorded for the people who would possess the promised land. If they failed to keep the Law and serve God, Yнwн would boot them out.

Thus, we have to see God as faithful to his Word in all things! We serve a God who never lies and always keeps his promises.

And even in discipline, he is thinking of restoration. Jeremiah and Ezekiel are littered with God's plans for rebuilding after a season of discipline. Jeremiah 29:11 comes to a people who are currently in a backslidden state as a hope on the day they awake to their senses in the middle of their desolation.

God is faithful.

MAKE A NOTE

_____

_____

_____

_____

_____

_____

_____

_____

_____

_____

_____

EZEKIEL 13
⬇
EZEKIEL 47

One of the most annoying features of technology is all the system updates. My battery always holds a smaller charge, there's always a learning curve with the new features and layouts, and then I have to update all the apps, or apps start bugging out because something in the update isn't communicating right.

But on the other hand, the system updates help my phone properly function in the ever-changing tech world I'm having to navigate every day. Imagine trying to use the internet today with an iPhone from 10 years ago: Safari would be chugging while it tries to load the Amazon splash page, none of the images would load, and the text would all be blue. Safari would then crash, and the phone would send a message that says, "This hurt my brain."

The prophet Ezekiel says the most amazing thing in 36:26-27: "I'm gonna give you a new operating system." (Nathan Finochio Version)

The human heart was chugging the entire time it was trying to load the Law of Moses.

The system would crash.

David found a hack: if I stay in the Spirit, my heart gets filled with love for God and his ways, and his ways are written in the Law of Moses.

Ezekiel points to a time in history—a time just around the corner—that God will update the human heart by creating a new heart, a clean heart (like David asked for in Psalm 51), by the work of the Holy Spirit in regeneration. Then the Holy Spirit comes to live inside of us, constantly doing all the updates for us.

The heart of the prophetic message of Ezekiel is this very thing. God has a bright future for us, and he's going to roll up his own sleeves and get busy doing the very thing that we cannot—serve him. It takes God to serve God. And that's the hack of the new covenant, a covenant where the indwelling Spirit of God is actually working in tandem with us to love the Lord with all our heart.

There is no pride that we can hide behind because we have a revelation that we actually deserve death. And at this revelation, we receive mercy—a new heart!

The result of the new operating system is a land promise—but a better land, the new heavens and new earth. Hebrews 11:10 tells us that the city Abraham was looking for was a heavenly city: a city God had designed.

Abraham was a city boy who lived in tents most of his life. The exilic community that Ezekiel is ministering to is doing just that: living in a temporary place in Babylon, longing for a city that is theirs. God will bring them back, but there's another people of God Ezekiel is speaking to—the New Testament Church. Perhaps that is precisely who Ezekiel is speaking to in an eschatological way.

The prophetic paradigm is like this: Ezekiel is ministering to a present audience in a terrible situation, and his prophecy about a new heart and corresponding land is for them. Yet by the Spirit, Ezekiel is also ministering to you and me right now in our situation, and perhaps even more so because we are the Israel of God (Galatians 6:16)—the Church—and his prophetic utterance about a new heart and the indwelling Spirit anticipates what God did by his Holy Spirit in Acts 2. Thus, Ezekiel is hitting two targets at once.

So we, like the people of Judah in Babylonian exile living in a temporary place, are all children of Abraham (the OG man of faith): a city boy who hated camping and wanted to live in a cozy west village apartment above an Italian restaurant with his cat, Meowssiah. Abraham never got his Manhattan wish because he got something better—life in a city designed by God himself. And the prize is that he got there. He "strived to enter that rest," as the author of Hebrews 4:11 suggests.

There is a promised land for every believer, and the Church is perhaps living like Abraham and Israel, in exile, but God has given us his Spirit, and he says, "Don't compromise. Stay devoted to me! I haven't left you alone. In fact, I've come to help you by living within you and bringing life to your spirit. And if you endure, I'll bring you into the land! Don't get cocky. Stay humble and trust me. I am preparing your dream future right now!"

MAKE A NOTE

I was watching a movie recently with my wife, and I predicted that life for the protagonist was about to get worse. She asked, "Why do you say that?"

To which I responded, "Because every good writer knows that the problem has to become a bigger problem in order to hook the audience and make a satisfying payoff." I was right.

As we enter the book of Daniel, we are already well equipped to understand this story. Daniel is a Judaean prince who has been selected for the re-education camps of the empire. The Babylonians (unlike their Assyrian counterparts) would repurpose rather than destroy the best parts of a society they had captured. This often meant rebuilding temples in order to garner favor with the local deities, or reorienting young foreign aristocrats into Babylonian culture and political life.

Other cultures held the same values as the Babylonians: gold, girls, and glory. But the princes of Judah ended up being different. They were ideologues who stuck out like a sore thumb in the syncretistic and multicultural melting pot that was Babylonia.

As we read about Daniel and his insistence on observing Kosher Law, we see this as an act of fidelity to Yhwh. When he refuses to bow down to Nebuchadnezzar's idol, we wonder where this kind of bravery was in the last several centuries. Even in regime change, Daniel stays afloat—clearly God is with him. Even a den of lions won't keep Daniel from obedience to Yhwh.

Daniel and his friends suffered psychological abuses: their names were changed to names that glorified Babylonian deities. One commentator suggests that they may have been castrated (as many were), further creating internal problems of God's acceptance of them (Leviticus 21:20) seeing as a eunuch couldn't enter the temple.[15]

Yet they stay loyal to Yhwh.

Imagine how this story would inspire the first hearers who just returned to Jerusalem from the exile. This is the hero that Ezra and Nehemiah want the young boys of Judah to pattern: a guy who singlehandedly defies the gods of Babylon, survives his enemies, and experiences the miraculous favor of Yhwh his entire life because of his covenant loyalty.

And yet with all the good stuff happening amongst the bad stuff, the book of Daniel somehow just gets creepier—or worse—in this apocalyptic psychological thriller sort of way. Satan, the Prince of Persia, angelic battles, war in heaven, Armageddon, the end of the age—it's pretty heavy stuff, like knowing Dad is coming home with the wooden spoon after he's done at work because you were a menace at school that day.

And while Daniel survives and ultimately thrives in this environment, because the hand of God is upon him and these empires fall as quickly as they rise, there is this gross darkness that continues to form and develop in the book. And I am referring to the dark spiritual forces that are behind the failures of Israel.

Israel has an enemy, and that enemy is the devil. As soon as God declared his love and fidelity toward his people, a target was immediately placed upon the nation. Satan is doing everything he can to trip them up and cut them down, and in Daniel, this comes to the forefront. Israel isn't just in a material battle, they are in a spiritual battle.

We are comforted in the apocalyptic visions of Daniel by the reality that the kingdom of God eventually conquers every other kingdom, vanquishing the power of darkness and their paid agitators.

So as we read Daniel, we are encouraged to find inspiration in his example of steadfastness under persecution, and we are blessed to find hope in God's ultimate victory in the cosmic war, even as we feel it brewing all around us in these uncertain times.

It is this very Sauron-like gathering of dark clouds in apocalyptic literature that makes me think God is the very best writer of human history because—knowing that he ultimately wins—the bad things that come will make the triumph that much sweeter.

MAKE A NOTE

OBADIAH 1
⬇
MALACHI 4

As we finish the Old Testament, we cruise through a mixed bag of short prophetic books, called the "Minor Prophets" because of the brevity of their writings, as opposed to the more long-winded major prophets who tended to keep people in church long after lunch time.

There's nothing minor about these prophets, however. These guys played just as large a role and sometimes even larger in the spiritual and political life of Israel. Jonah is a unique book in this collection because he's a prophet to Nineveh—the capital city of the Assyrian Empire—Israel's nemesis.

Jonah doesn't like the idea of ministering to Nineveh because he hates the Assyrians, and he knows that God will forgive them if they repent. The book of Jonah is more about God saving Jonah than Jonah saving Nineveh, and it teaches us that what God has called us to is paradoxically saving us. Jonah is backslidden himself, and his body is just catching up to his runaway heart. His salvation moment in the belly of the whale is incredible: he's given up hope for living, but he begins to worship. God hears him from heaven and demonstrates his character—the same character that Jonah doesn't want God to show toward Nineveh. This book is equal parts narrative theology and comedy.

The last three books of this reading section are my favorites because they are building books. Haggai, Zechariah, and Malachi are ministering to the returned exiles who are rebuilding Jerusalem from the ashes. They are fresh upon the scene after the devastation of the tornado, picking up the pieces of their precious city. Will God help them? Is there a future for them? What are the secrets of success? And is God pleased? What are the spiritual challenges?

These prophets don't pull any punches, especially Malachi. Eileen Schuller observes, "Modern understanding of prophecy has tended to be much more sympathetic to the voice of Amos and finds it very difficult to incorporate Malachi into a 'working definition' of prophecy."[16]

Amos wants justice to roll down like a river. I can quote him on my picket sign as a mark of divine blessing. Amos approves of anything and everything I call justice; it's very convenient.

Malachi gets specific about justice—too specific. He's quoting the Law. Paradoxically, Malachi opens up by the Lord saying, "I have loved you" (Malachi 1:2).

Israel responds, perhaps with a sneer, "How have you loved us?"[17]

God goes, "I rejected everyone else and chose you!" Then he gets into specifics. "You say you love me, and you are going to be better than those losers who got kicked out of the land, but you are cutting corners everywhere you can with your love."

The offerings from the people are terrible—blind animals, lame animals, sick animals. I'm laughing because it's hilarious that these morons are trying to get the blessing of God's presence but give God "a special present" of a blind cow in a wheelchair with cancer. "He's got like eight minutes to live. Enjoy!"

God's like, "If you gave that to anybody else would they be happy?"

The priests teach horrible theology, the men marry foreigners who are idolators and raise their kids to worship the foreign gods of the foreign women, and the nation refuses to tithe. Men are divorcing their wives because they don't love them anymore. God is disgusted. He notices who is convicted by these words, and he tells the people that he's making a book of remembrance, recording all the names of the ones who repent.

Then the book ends with a promise that God will send Elijah the prophet, who will "turn the hearts of fathers to their children and the hearts of children to their fathers" (Malachi 4:5-6) so the nation can mend their ways and avoid national disaster.

As we read through the New Testament, we see the prophetic scope of this word, having its fulfillment both in the nation but also in the church.

MAKE A NOTE

Congratulations! You finished the Old Testament!

That's massive, but your work is just beginning: you can't waste all the knowledge you have accumulated now. You are actually primed to see all these stories crescendo in the coming of the main character—Jesus Christ, the Messiah—the Seed of the Woman, the Suffering Servant, the Son of David, the Messiah, the Holy One of Israel, the Great High Priest, the Blessing of Abraham, the Better Temple with a better altar and better sacrifices and a better priesthood!

Matthew is writing to a mainly Jewish audience, and his chief goal is to show that Jesus is a fulfillment to the Scriptures—the primary source documents that shape this Jewish audience.

The Scriptures weren't just an important book to this culture; they were the center of all social and political life. They were the Jewish people's identity. So when Matthew starts telling the story of Jesus of Nazareth and says, "This was to fulfill this Scripture and that Scripture," the audience's ears are perking up. Matthew will use language that will immediately recall other stories to the hearers.

And that's the point of reading the Old Testament: to recall stories and poetry and prophetic utterances and historical realities and themes that make God's purposes for humanity immediately recognizable in Jesus Christ.

As you read Matthew today, allow his Gospel to bring to mind things you read in the last 23 days. Perhaps some of it will whizz by your head. Keep in mind that the first hearers had put the entirety of Isaiah and Psalms to memory by the time they were 13. These people knew their own story better than any culture that has ever existed because of the corporate traumas they had experienced.

They are afraid for their nation. They are living in the Roman province of Judea now. The occupiers march the streets, giving them the feeling of Babylon come to Jerusalem, and a denial of their Jewishness in any form would be considered turning their back on their nation and Yhwh.

So Matthew, a former tax-collector turncoat, has to carefully ground the story of Jesus in the world of the Law and the Prophets. Jesus must be seen as the fulfillment of Scripture, not some random dude creating a new form of spirituality.

Many Christians fail to see how important the Old Testament is as proof of Jesus' deity for various reasons, sometimes because they think the Old Testament is just a bunch of archaic rules and violent national stories, or because the God of the Old Testament is a monster and thus the Israelite authors fumbled the message, or because they haven't read the Scriptures.

You have a unique advantage today as a reader: the advantage of the disciples of Jesus. They knew the Old Testament inside and out, and when they met Jesus, and as he opened the Scriptures to them and lived out the power of his life and calling, they were convinced beyond a shadow of a doubt that Jesus was exactly who Moses and David and the prophets predicted by the Holy Spirit.

As you read Matthew and the beginning of Mark today, allow yourself to recall the backdrop of salvation history. Paint it in your imagination so the story of Jesus comes alive in a fresh way.

MAKE A NOTE

_____

_____

_____

_____

_____

_____

_____

_____

_____

_____

_____

_____

_____

_____

_____

MARK 6
→
LUKE 15

My favorite kind of movie is action. Don't bore us, get to the chorus. I want to see explosions, shells littering the ground, and all the bad guys dead. And this is why Mark is my second favorite Gospel writer (my favorite is John). I love the genre—action.

Sometimes referred to as Peter's Gospel by church fathers (Papias, Irenaeus) and scholars alike, it is possible that Mark—being a travel companion of Peter—collected the pericope (isolated little stories) of Peter as he preached and then assembled them later like a journalist or biographer.[18]

The idea is that Peter is at the pub telling all these crazy stories like an Irish rover, each one more incredulous than the next, and Mark is beside him, feverishly writing down Peter's ramblings on bar napkins. Later, Mark will assemble the napkins and piece together this monster, but he will allow Peter's style of storytelling (the historic present) to come through—a rough style of Greek that reflects the personality of the fisherman.[19] Perhaps this style of Gospel would connect with your blue-collar worker who prefers action to the snooty sophistry of Luke or Jewish mindfulness of Matthew. Thus, the formation of this book hears better than it reads because it wasn't written by a writer for readers but preached by a preacher for average Joes: people who were steeped in and preferred oral tradition.[20]

The use of *immediately* (42 times; in the other Gospels collectively only six) sets the tone. Paradoxically, as "immediately" as the disciples start following Jesus, they abandon him.

Mark doesn't shy away from the failures and heartbreak of this story either. Good action flicks have to be a little gritty. As you read, watch for the failure of the disciples, and notice that Jesus is pretty much suffering and alone at the very end. Mark's Gospel could almost be seen as ending on a cliff-hanger.

I find comfort in the failure of the disciples and probably identify with Peter more than I would with Paul. The three boat scenes (4:35-41; 6:45-52; 8:14-21), the three times the disciples fall asleep at Gethsemane (14:37, 40, 41), and Peter's three denials of Jesus (14:66-72) all underline how faithless they were.[21] Mark is intentional about recording Peter's story this way; perhaps because Peter doesn't want people to think of him as a hero, but rather as a vessel of grace. Peter's restoration isn't even in Mark; it's in John! And yet Jesus loves Peter.

Somebody has to be a grownup and make a significant literary contribution to both the world of literature on behalf of the Hellenized Age as well as make the Bible look excellent to the academics, and that's where Dr. Luke comes in, writing some of the finest Greek in the New Testament.[22] His Gospel is the first of a two-volume report on Christianity. Luke is also the author of Acts. In the Gospel of Luke, perhaps the author will survey Mark and Matthew's narrative contributions and then add research that he's done as well.

While Mark's audience appears to be a Roman one, Luke's audience appears to be a Greek-speaking one. And because most of the world spoke Greek at this time, Luke's letter will spread across the known world, informing everyone that Jesus is the Savior for all people.

Although Luke will include some packaging his Greek audience would appreciate—a hero birth story from the maternal point of view, the revelation of Christ in the garden that echoes the words of Orestes to Electra,[23] the son presumed dead and unrecognized by his sister now home to right wrongs—Luke is fully immersed in the story of Israel and their need for Messiah.

One commentator has suggested that Luke's narrative style copies the Old Testament language and structure so well that he continues the Greek Old Testament, even down to patterning his Gospel after the Elijah-Elisha narrative.[24]

Luke is freakishly literate, and his Greek education coupled with his Jewish grasp of the Scriptures makes reading his Gospel incredibly palatable.

While Luke is setting up a detailed report on the life and ministry of Christ, he is establishing a beachhead for the story and ministry of the Holy Spirit in this rapid-growth social movement called *Christianity*, comprised of the Church.

The Church is a new social idea that is catching like wildfire all over the Mediterranean. Luke is going to give some context to his readers on what Christians are all about.

The Holy Spirit is a feature in the life of Jesus of Nazareth—note the work of the Spirit in Luke 3-4. When Luke drops Acts, the next book, the reader is all caught up on this Jesus thing and starts to understand how the Holy Spirit is the next iteration of God fully alive and living in the newly formed Jesus community.[25]

MAKE A NOTE

_____

_____

_____

_____

_____

_____

_____

_____

_____

_____

One of my favorite Disney movie scenes to reference is that part in *Ratatouille* when Remy bites a bit of grape and a bit of cheese with his eyes closed, and all of a sudden, it's fireworks over Cinderella's castle.

That's what happens to my brain when I'm shredding and I start reading the Gospels: all that grape of the Law of Moses and Davidic history mixed with the sharp, aged cheese of Psalms and the Prophets causes a Gandalf-style explosion over Hobbiton in my brain.

Luke is no exception: Luke's central theme of the arrival of God's salvation plan for all people, supported by a realization of Ezekiel and Joel's Spirit power and Isaiah's vision of Yнwн's power over the human history, as well as "all nations" pouring into Yнwн's house, creates atmospheres of biblical fulfillment in such a short amount of time.

The prophets were like "this is coming, this is coming, get ready," and then Jesus just escalates and fulfills long-awaited, snail-paced prophecies in three short years of ministry.

I call it the Jesus Ka-boom.

The current leadership aren't here for it, but that's sort of typical of Israel, who miss their time of visitation and kill the prophets because they get caught up in the same pride issues that Ezekiel was addressing. They end up murdering Jesus—who is completely innocent—but he comes back from the dead and gets straight back to business on the road to Emmaus, opening up the Scriptures and using these sacred texts as proof of his Messianic identity. Jesus is continually coming after lost people in Luke.

John is the last Gospel and perhaps one of the last New Testament books written. John has lived long enough to hear people's pushbacks on the other Gospel writers, so he decides to weigh in on the Jesus story as Jesus' best friend—no big deal. (John continually reminds us of that in his Gospel; see if you can spot it.)

Matthew, Mark, and Luke are called the *Synoptics* by biblical scholars because they share a lot of the same material in their retelling of the Jesus story. John is gonna drop his tell-all using material that is 90% unique to the Synoptics: all new stories, all new miracles, all new sayings of Jesus. This is the best friend journal, the exclusive interview, that John has been sitting on all these years.

One of the criticisms of the Greeks is that there's no way Jesus could be fully God and fully man at the same time. Plato taught them that matter is bad and spirit is good, and those two things are like oil and water. They don't mix.

John starts his Gospel as a polemic against these Gnostic believers who prefer a pseudo-Jesus spirituality that is buffet-style, requires zero physical engagement or embodiment, and remains in the realm of the metaphysic.

John's like, "Bro, in the beginning was the Word. That's Jesus' code name, and Jesus is God. And the Word became flesh; we watched him eat fish. I saw those nails go in, man. You don't know what you're talking about. I saw this. I was an eyewitness to this, genius."

Eyewitness testimony was a huge deal in the ancient world and considered the most reliable form of a historical document.[26] John self-describes as one of the many people who witnessed Jesus, a surviving voice of legal testimony.

Story after story will illustrate the humanity of Jesus: his first miracle being at an awkward family wedding where his mom pulls rank in order to save face for the embarrassed couple who run out of wine. Jesus asks John to take care of this same annoying mom as he's dying on a tree. He weeps. He cooks fish for breakfast and eats it in his resurrected body, giving further proof that the Greek philosophic paradigm of heaven and earth is obliterated by the Christian vision of eternity.

In the other Gospels, Jesus is holding a lamb and saying nice things. In John, you just wandered into Jesus' neighborhood, and he will cut you. Zero punches are pulled with respect to the demands of discipleship. You wanna follow Jesus? Cool. Die. Take up your cross. Oh, and you have no other options. The "I am" statements appear exclusively in John. (See if you can count how many there are as you read through it.) Jesus purposely stands in the way of manipulative, self-manifesting spirituality here. He says that he is the only way to the Father, "the way, and the truth, and the life" (John 14:6), and other such single-lane analogies.

Jesus' longest prayer is also recorded in John 17. Perhaps John is suggesting that while Peter was sleeping, he was listening, reminding the Lord gently that he was *mostly* awake that night he got lumped in with Peter the denier.

John is cheeky, genius, decisive, selective, and truthful in his Gospel, and I love the portrait he presents of Jesus, particularly in John 21—perhaps my favorite passage of the entire New Testament—where Jesus is having awkward conversations, sticking to a caveman diet, and messing with his disciples all the while loving them.

MAKE A NOTE

_____

_____

_____

_____

_____

_____

_____

_____

_____

ACTS 3
⬇
ROMANS 8

The book of Acts could be called the Book of the Holy Spirit or the Book of the Church, as these themes feature so prominently throughout. Luke has just finished telling the story of Jesus of Nazareth in his Gospel, and he turns his attention to the last words of Christ before his ascension: go wait in Jerusalem until the promised Holy Spirit shows up.

The disciples are portrayed at the beginning of the book as puzzled. They're still asking about national political revival. Isn't that what the prophets had been prophesying about? When are we gonna kick these Romans out and restore the kingdom of David?

Jesus deflates back to earth, mid-takeoff, like a balloon losing air, shaking his head and telling the boys, "Guys, are you kidding me right now? My kingdom is not of this world. I've been saying that over and over again."

"Well that's nice, but don't leave us. If we don't have you to lead us, we are up a creek without a paddle!"

"The Holy Spirit is on his way. He's going to rock your little worlds. If you liked my bag of tricks, just wait 'til you see this dude's firepower."

And that's exactly what happens. Peter the wimp turns into Peter Beast-mode. Saul the persecutor turns into Paul the Apostle. The Holy Spirit works staggering transformation on these guys. And guidance? Before the Holy Spirit shows up, they're drawing sticks to figure out who the new apostle will be. After he shows up, they have dreams, visions, prophetic utterances, and defined purpose.

As is the case with Luke, he masterfully lays out the story of how the gospel got all the way to the heart of the Empire—Rome. The book is filled with this massive theme of parallel between Peter and Paul[27]— the Jerusalem Church and the Gentile Church—and will help give future church leaders background on the theological and practical development of the Christian ethos.

Christians can read this book and know that God is with them powerfully by the Holy Spirit, opening up opportunities for the gospel to be preached all over the world.

As we open up Romans, it's important to track with Paul immediately in chapter one, where he's gonna throw around some pretty huge ideas that will form a foundation for the next eight chapters. This is where he lays out how sinners can become righteous in the greatest detail in all of the New Testament.

This is Paul's magnum opus.

Two realities are being revealed in Paul's Gospel that tend to be competing ideas in our heads and hearts at times, but Paul will juxtapose them in chapter one: the righteousness of God that is being revealed and the wrath of God that is being revealed.

The righteousness of God is revealed from faith to faith (from what God has done in salvation history to what God is doing now in Christ Jesus), but the wrath of God is also being revealed (from what God has revealed about himself in Scripture and at the revelation of Christ Jesus).

Most of us love the righteousness-by-faith part, but we bristle at the idea of God's wrath, so let's see if we can understand it better.

God is not experiencing the irrational passion of anger, flying off the handle at sinners in a capricious rage like the Greek gods. He is thoroughly rational and totally justified in his higher wrath—a wrath you and I can't comprehend because in our wrath the presence of sin is always in us. In fact, if God isn't angry at the holocaust or the Armenian genocide or chattel slavery, he would be guilty of failure to love his creation.[28]

God is rightfully and perfectly angry at what sin is doing to humans, how humans are sinning against other humans, and how humanity has rejected him and decided to become like the animal gods they worship in their thinking and behavior. Salvation and wrath are simultaneously being rolled out. God is actively working in the world.

In Romans 1, we see the Gentiles being judged. In Romans 2, we see the Jews being judged because they are relying on Ezekiel's pillars of pride to save them, yet they break the Law constantly. In Romans 3, Paul summarizes that we are all being judged—all of us—because we have all sinned and fall short of the glory of God. But the good news is that we can be righteous by faith in Christ Jesus.

Paul will then build a biblical case for righteousness by faith, in Chapter 4, by explaining what Yʜwʜ did in his covenant with Abraham. The Jews listening in to the conversation will be encouraged to abandon all their pride and reduce their spirituality to Abraham's—the father of faith who wasn't circumcised and didn't have the Law of Moses but was made righteous by faith.

Romans is more *Ratatouille* brain explosions as you begin to see the stories you've just read come alive!

MAKE A NOTE

_____

_____

_____

_____

_____

_____

_____

_____

_____

_____

The perpetual thorn in Paul's side throughout his missionary journey was the Judaizers, a group of Jewish Christians who insisted that the Gentile Christians practice the Law of Moses. They demanded that the Gentiles be circumcised, follow kosher law, and practice sabbath and many other traditions peripheral to the gospel.

There was another side to the frustrations however. Antisemitism raged throughout the Roman Empire. The Jews had been expelled from Rome twice in the last 50 years, once by Tiberius in A.D. 19 and recently by Claudius in A.D. 46. The Gentile Christians were starting to get sick of the Judaizers and their relentless complaining, and they began to hit back.

The Roman and Galatian church had become ethnically divided over kosher law, so the Lord's

Supper couldn't be celebrated. Paul's methodical laying out of the gospel is how he brings healing to these churches.

He will tell the Galatians that there is no Jew or Greek in Christ, meaning that nobody has a leg up. Yes, these cultural differences exist, but we can't carry them into the Body and start demanding accommodation. It's not what saves us, and it's not what unites us. Christ unites us—period.

The Corinthians are the worst church in the Bible, and it's not even close. Their services are a dumpster fire. Paul tells them in 1 Corinthians 11:17 that it's actually worse when they gather. Imagine a church so bad that you feel worse for going.

God's presence is still among them, but the cup of blessing is turning into the cup of judgment because of their total disregard for Christ and one another. They are making church all about themselves. In doing so, Paul tells them that God is gonna destroy them (1 Corinthians 3) if they keep destroying the temple of the Lord—the collective body of believers. Tom Schreiner recalls the Achan narrative: those who destroy the church are touching what is holy and sacred, and God will destroy them.[29]

Then in Second Corinthians, Paul has to beg them not to follow self-proclaimed apostles who are Cretans and liars. The fact that Paul writes these people letters is a miracle in itself.

The church at Corinth made the fatal mistake of bringing their Corinthian culture—a wild, selfish, sensual, unredeemed, and ungodly culture—into the Church. They are highly gifted and charismatic but show zero spiritual maturity or Spirit-fruited-ness. The gifts are immediate, the fruit takes time; the gifts are free, the fruit is costly.

The Ephesians are going to become the best church in the New Testament. John the Apostle will eventually move there, and Timothy will take over for John as lead elder. The beginnings of the Church are tough. Members are severely persecuted because Christianity poses an existential threat to the trade guild, and the locals consider the Diana worship business to be the reason the city is so prosperous. When Ephesians became Christians and received the mark of God, they were thrown out of the trade guild and found it difficult to buy and sell. Perhaps this specific local experience is what John will refer to in his apocalypse.

The Ephesians need a vision of what they are a part of—that giant temple of Diana is intimidating and takes up a lot of space in their psychology. Paul will paint a beautiful picture of the Church for the Ephesians that will ultimately stir and ground their hearts in what God is doing in and among them.

MAKE A NOTE

_____

_____

_____

_____

_____

_____

_____

_____

_____

_____

PHILIPPIANS 1
⬇
1 PETER 2

This is where the Shred starts to annoy those who are more pedantic. You're gonna read 10 books of the Bible today. Thankfully, all but one are written by Paul, and Paul tends to have similar emphases. Paul is a pastor of a lot of churches, and each congregation presents unique challenges.

The Philippians are a wealthy congregation from a snooty Roman colony made up of successful retirees. The Colossians are primarily Greek, living in a forgotten town where industry had all but left for a neighboring town. The Philippians are instructed not to get cocky about their citizenship to Rome but remember it's in heaven; don't get too close to your earthly accomplishment. The Colossians are reminded that God the Father qualified them and added them to the family. Even though once they were alienated from him, God hasn't forgotten them. He knows exactly where they are on the map of his purposes.[30]

The Thessalonians are the conspiracy theorists of the New Testament, obsessed with the return of Christ, and have stopped working because they think it's any day now. Paul has to tell them to stop posting on Facebook every time Russia does something and get a job.

Paul will write three very personal pastoral letters to two young men he is mentoring—Timothy and Titus. Note how many times Paul tells them to pay attention to their doctrine and teaching. He also wants them to organize their churches in a prophetic way that sticks to the Bible and confronts the lunacy of the cultures in which they find themselves, not like those maniac Corinthians who run their churches like a local brothel.

Social order is a big deal for Paul because it creates cultural cohesion for the churches, which is hard enough seeing as everyone is from a completely different background and brings in all kinds of experiential baggage.

Philemon is a masterclass in rhetoric. Paul is writing on behalf of a runaway slave to his master. Both of them are Christians, further complicating things. What will Philemon do: kill his slave, or welcome him home as a brother? Roman Law allowed a slave owner to execute the rest of the slaves if a slave ran away! And how does Christianity alter the socio-economic topography of a church? Paul doesn't come out and ban Philemon from being a slave owner, but he is demanding that Philemon rethink what that looks like, and perhaps it's something Philemon wants to participate in, given that everything in Christ changes us. The gospel has implications!

The book of Hebrews is written to Jewish Christians struggling with their faith. Their friends and family raise some great points: How can you worship God if you don't have Moses, the temple, the priesthood, the altar, or the sacrifices? Plus, nobody is doing business with you, and you've been completely ostracized from your community. Hebrews will take down all these arguments and encourage the discouraged Christians to stick with Jesus because he's better than Moses: his priesthood is better, his altar is better, and the sacrifices are better!

James is sick of people who say they know Jesus but act like they don't. He doesn't like how people are abusing

Paul's message of faith and grace. James' message is, "If you really have faith, your life will be full of proof!"

As you read today, consider how these unique messages round each other out and balance the extremes that people tend to gravitate toward.

MAKE A NOTE

_____

_____

_____

_____

_____

_____

_____

_____

_____

_____

_____

_____

_____

_____

If you're reading this, you are on your last day of the Shred, and that means you've done what most Christians have never done in their lifetime: you've read the entire Bible—and read it like a book.

The Bible read as a whole book is much more rewarding than nibbled at in isolated parts, and the reason being should be obvious by now: it is its own reference point. The further you read through it, the more you see this intertextuality at work.

This last day of reading is no exception: Peter, Jude and John will expand upon the work of the prophetic writers, some second temple authors who offer apocalyptic language for Peter and Jude, and the apocalypse of Daniel. This inter-connectedness of Scripture and the expansion of Peter, Jude, and John into New Testament apocalypse is profound. It tells us two things: 1) they knew they were writing Scripture, and 2) they knew God was going to wrap up time with a sizzle—exactly how the prophets forewarned.

Now the end of the Bible, like the end of the Old Testament, is a cliffhanger with some pretty troubling notes—the soundtrack isn't Tchaikovsky's "1812 Overture," but rather Sondheim's "Sweeney Todd"—and like any good story, the bad situation needs to get worse so the victory is all-time. Yes, we win if we stay faithful to the end just as Jesus was faithful to the end. Knowing how the book ends gives us perspective, but we aren't guaranteed smooth sailing.

The purpose of books like Revelation is to encourage us to stick with Jesus no matter what. As we read Revelation, we can be comforted by the reality that the Holy Spirit himself will give us the power and animated endurance in the middle of suffering that will amaze even us.[31]

Sandwiched in between Peter, Jude, and Revelation are John's pastoral letters where he gives us the hitchhiker's guide to surviving the apocalypse: remaining in the love of God, as John explains in his Gospel (John 15). Jude also drops this hint (1:20-23). Staying in the love of God is the key to faithful witness, and that is done by praying in the Spirit. Jesus is the wisdom of God (Proverbs 8), and the Holy Spirit is the love of God (Romans 5:5). By praying in the Spirit, we are remaining in the love of God, and it is only by the power of the Spirit that we can hope to remain faithful witnesses to Jesus Christ in a world that is openly hostile to the things of God.

As you finish your reading today, observe how much of these authors' world is informed by the reading you just did this month, and allow the congruence and prophetic continuity of Scripture to build your faith in God's ability to be faithful to you in your world and cultural context.

God knows your name. He sees you coming close to him in this reading. And he is the one who has been drawing you to himself—even in this reading plan. In the same way he was ordering human history, he's ordering your steps. He's a God who is close and not far off. When you step toward him, he runs toward you.

My prayer is that the Holy Spirit tattoos some of the verses that you've read on your heart—words that will get you to where you need to be in Christ Jesus—in the coming days. Amen.

MAKE A NOTE

ENDNOTES

1   G.K. Chesterton, *"Democracy and Physical Science"*
    (Illustrated London News, November 23, 1907)

2   Michael S. Heiser, *The Unseen Realm* (Bellingham: WA,
    Lexham Press, 2015), pg. 13

3   Mark L. Strauss, *Four Portraits, One Jesus* (Grand Rapids:
    MI, Zondervan, 2007), pg. 19

4   Bruce K. Waltke, *An Old Testament Theology* (Grand Rapids:
    MI, Zondervan, 2007), pp. 46-48

5   J. Gordon McConville, *Grace in the End: A Study in
    Deuteronomic Theology* (Grand Rapids: MI, Zondervan,
    1993), pg. 9

6   Michael S. Heiser, *The Unseen Realm,* p.188

7   Michael Heiser, *I Dare You Not to Bore Me with the Bible*
    (Bellingham, WA: Lexham Press, 2014), pp. 67-69

8   Holy Bible, *New International Version,* Psalm 150:6

9   Gordon D. Fee, Douglas Stuart, *How to Read the Bible for
    All Its Worth* (Grand Rapids: MI, Zondervan, 2003), pg. 238

10 Gordon D. Fee, Douglas Stuart, *How to Read the Bible for
    All Its Worth,* pg. 237

11 Joseph Blenkinsopp, *Isaiah 56-66: The Anchor Yale Bible*
    (New York: NY, Doubleday, 2003), pg. 90

12 Walter A. Elwell, *Baker Encyclopedia of the Bible* (Grand
    Rapids: MI, Baker Book House Company, 1988), pg. 1111

13 Daniel I. Block, *Beyond the River Chebar: Studies in Kingship
    and Eschatology in the Book of Ezekiel* (Eugene: OR, Cascade
    Books, 2013), pg. 9

14 Daniel I. Block, *Beyond the River Chebar,* pg. 7

15 Tremper Longman III, *How to Read Daniel* (Downers
    Grove: IL, Intervarsity Press, 2020), pg. 146

16 Eileen M. Schuller, *Malachi: New Interpreters Bible Commentary* (Nashville: TN, Abingdon Press, 2004), pg. 861

17 Elizabeth Achtemeier, *Nahum - Malachi* (Atlanta: GA, John Knox, 1986), pg. 174

18 Ben Witherington III, *The Gospel of Mark* (Grand Rapids: MI, Eerdmans, 2001), pg. 22

19 Mark L. Strauss, *Four Portraits: One Jesus* (Grand Rapids: MI, Zondervan, 2007), pg. 174

20 Antoinette Clark Wire, *The Case for Mark Composed in Performance* (Eugene: OR, Cascade, 2011), pg. 4

21 Strauss, *Four Portraits*, pg. 177

22 Strauss, *Four Portraits*, pg. 262

23 Sophocles, *Electra*

24 Thomas L. Brodie, *The Crucial Bridge. The Elijah-Elisha Narrative as an Interpretive Synthesis of Genesis-Kings and a Literary Model for the Gospels* (Collegeville: MN: Liturgical Press, 2000), esp. pp. 29-78

25 Gordon D. Fee, Douglas Stuart, *How to Read the Bible Book by Book* (Grand Rapids: MI, Zondervan, 2002), pg. 298

26 Richard Bauckham, *Jesus and the Eyewitness: The Gospels as Eyewitness Testimony* (Grand Rapids: MI, Eerdmans, 2006), pp. 8-10

27 James D.G. Dunn, *The Acts of the Apostles* (Grand Rapids: MI, Eerdmans, 1996), pg. 14

28 C.E.B. Cranfield, *A Critical and Exegetical Commentary on the Epistle to the Romans, Volume 1* (London: UK, T&T Clark, 1975), pg. 109

29   Thomas R. Schreiner, *1 Corinthians* (Downers Grove: IL, IVP Academic, 2018), pg. 94

30   Douglas J. Moo, *The Letters to the Colossians and to Philemon* (Grand Rapids: MI, Eerdmans, 2008), pg. 27

31   Chris M. Palmer, "Suffering and Theodicy in the Apocalypse: A Pentecostal Exploration" (PhD Thesis, Bangor University, 2024) pg. 94

ABOUT THE AUTHOR

Nathan Finochio is the founder of TheosU and TheosSeminary, innovative online platforms dedicated to teaching faithful biblical theology. With a passion for truth and clarity in biblical education, Nathan has gained recognition as a global speaker, addressing audiences on theological issues across continents. He serves as the teaching pastor at Holy Saints Franklin, where he resides.

Nathan's academic journey began at Portland Bible College in Portland, OR, where he earned his Bachelor of Theology. He later pursued advanced studies, obtaining a Master of Arts in Theological Studies from Southeastern University. His commitment to deepening others' understanding of faith is reflected in his written works, including the widely read *Hearing God* and the influential *Killer Church*.

Beyond his teaching and writing, Nathan maintains an active online presence, where his insights and teachings continue to reach a broad audience. Follow him at @nathanfinochio or visit his website at www.nathanfinochio.ca.